T0356698

Black.
Fat.
Femme.

Jonathan P. Higgins, Ed.D.

Black.
Fat.
Femme.

Revealing the Power of
Visibly Queer Voices
iN media
and Learning to Love Yourself

FOREWORD BY **Latrice Royale** *RuPaul's Drag Race* and
Host of HBO's *We're Here*

WILEY

Published by John Wiley & Sons, Inc., Hoboken, New Jersey.
Published simultaneously in Canada.

For general information on our other products and services or for technical support, please contact our Customer Care Department within the United States at (800) 762-2974, outside the United States at (317) 572-3993 or fax (317) 572-4002.

Wiley also publishes its books in a variety of electronic formats. Some content that appears in print may not be available in electronic formats. For more information about Wiley products, visit our web site at www.wiley.com.

Library of Congress Cataloging-in-Publication Data is available:

ISBN: 9781394296361 (cloth)
ISBN: 9781394296378 (ePub)
ISBN: 9781394296385 (ePDF)

Cover Design: Paul McCarthy
Cover Photo: Sequoia Emmanuelle Photography

SKY10099162_030125

For Loretta, Matt, and Carla.

Thank you for being my guardian angels. <3

Contents

Foreword   *ix*

Introduction: *Black, Fat, and Different*   *1*

1 **Always Too Much**   **15**

2 **The Chiffon Chronicles**   **35**

3 **The Making of a Queen**   **59**

4 **The Masc You Live In**   **81**

5 **Five Gs, Please!**   **101**

6 **To Be Loved**   **121**

7 **Becoming That B*tch**   **139**

8 **Redefining Authenticity**   **159**

9 **Remaining Black, Fat, and Visibly Queer**   **179**

10 **Yes, Black. Yes, Fat. Yes, Femme.**   **197**

Acknowledgments   *207*

About the Author   *213*

Index   *215*

Foreword

I can't begin to tell you *all* of the ways this title has resonated within me, but let me try.

Growing up as a little kid in Compton, California, presented its own set of problems. Being a "queer kid" was an entirely different situation. We don't have *gay* people in da hood! Imagine a time when gang violence was at an all-time high, along with the "War on Drugs" movement in full effect. There was nothing like me around, and I surely didn't have any interest in participating in the options available to me.

It was either gangs or the military – that's it!

Being the youngest of five boys, it was clear to my mother at this point that she did not want the same life for me, as my older brothers. She wanted me to have access to different tools and different cultures. My mother knew I was different from her other children; that's why she called me her "special child."

Once I started junior high school, my mother had figured out a way to get me out of Compton schools. I would be attending school in Long Beach, California, with a kaleidoscope of ethnicities and plenty of artistic tools to play with. What I was not ready for was the torment of being so different that I still felt like I didn't fit or belong. Here I am, this little chubby Black kid from Compton, using someone else's address so I can be in a new school, with no friends or people I even knew. This hardly seemed like a better way.

I've known from a very young age that I was "different" than the boys around me. I'd prefer to play Barbie with the girls and do hair, rather than play Tonka trucks and sports with the boys. I was more sensitive and a "mama's boy." These are the things that stuck out to me.

Evolving and developing throughout the years has taught me a kind of self-love that is impenetrable. It took a long time for me to understand the messages my mother was trying to instill in me as a youth. When I was being called names and made fun of because of my size, my mom simply said, "It's not what you're called; it's what you answer to, Son." I didn't get it! I was not feeling supported. But as I got older, I began to get it, and this light bulb finally came on. See, she was teaching me all along to never give people power over me. To keep that power, you have to accept and love everything about you . . . flaws and all.

And if there was something you didn't like about yourself, then it was up to you to change it! I would carry this mantra with me for the rest of my days.

Flash forward to the year 2012, when I appeared on the now multi-Emmy-Award–winning show called *RuPaul's Drag Race*. I auditioned just like many others, however, I was on a special mission. Operation Rebuild My Life was in motion! I went on the show with the intention of being fully myself, authentic, and completely transparent. I had lived, made a ton of mistakes, and had a wealth of knowledge based on real-life experiences. I shared freely and openly, and the world received me with open arms. Little did I know that I would strike such a chord with people! People from all over the world started sending messages of love, support, and gratitude for just sharing my story.

There was one particular person that I would always see tweets and DMs from. They would make sure nobody had anything bad to say about Miss Latrice! She was a beacon to them, a force, a light! I made sure I always acknowledged and responded to their messages and posts. We kept in touch from afar through the years, but when the opportunity came, they made sure to see me up close and in person!

It was the inaugural RuPaul's DragCon 2015, and fans flooded the Los Angeles Convention Center to meet their favorite queens from the franchise. After waiting for quite some time, the time had come for us to finally meet face-to-face. They introduce themselves as JonPaul from Twitter. And of course I remember you! We hugged like long-lost cousins! For me, this is what real love is – this is family!

At this point I have no clue about this person's life, what they've been through, or how they've gotten to this place of peace with who they are. As for me, I try to be as authentic and transparent as I possibly can. It helps me to stay on course by living my truth! I never thought about how that would resonate with others. I had clearly touched on some things that JonPaul and I have in common.

Both of us grew up in environments where our biggest bullies were inside the house. We had to navigate through those difficult years where we felt all alone because we knew we were different. Yet, in "Black culture," homosexuality is *not* a thing or option. When you couple that with religion, we have more layers of being ostracized and dismissed before we are even fully aware of our own sexuality. We are taught from an early age that God hates gays.

I started to struggle quite a bit with these teachings. As I grew older and was able to interpret things for myself, that's what ultimately led me to leave the church entirely. My findings could not make sense of the nonsense! I simply did not understand why there were so many different variations of the Bible.

Why did it say one thing and then the opposite in the next book or version? Not one person could help me understand, and no one could explain it to me, which made me raise more eyebrows and more questions. There was no doubt about it; I was just as confused as the people who were trying to preach to me about God's word. It would be several years until I would resolve my very personal relationship with my Higher Power.

I prayed to be released from the shame and guilt that I had carried with me for the entirety of my adult life up until that point. I wanted to learn to love myself. I wanted to find love. Once I learned step one, everything else would fall into place. It was as if I waved a magical wand . . . I didn't know how attractive confidence and happiness were! People have always gravitated toward me in general, so making friends has never been a problem. But romantically speaking, there wasn't really a market for the Black Fat Femme guy.

"Couldn't get any worse," one would think. Ha! I decided that I *loved* being a drag queen! Is this some kind of self-sabotage; is this my inner saboteur? So now I'm back to square one it seems. I have something that I love to do, but I am also ashamed. I couldn't let an inkling of drag be seen or heard of when trying to date, or to just hook up and get laid. It was not as popular in those times to date a queen.

Guys had a "type" . . . and I was not it! How do I relearn to love myself with this extension of my personality? It worked before, so let's start from step one. It would prove to be more difficult than expected. Gender identity issues enter the party. Ugh! What am I questioning all of a sudden? Why am I freaking out? The more I started to develop my drag character, the more people started to recognize me in and out of drag.

The issue was, I was not comfortable being referred to as "Latrice" out of drag. I definitely would be offended to be called Tim while in drag. Again, I still didn't want any potential suitors to know that I was a drag queen. I had a lot to unpack! Like I said, I went back to step one, and all else fell right into place. I became comfortable and secure in my gender identity. I knew I was a man, and I never had the feeling or thought of ever transitioning. I was out and proud again, loving all of me! It took time and work to get to this place, and I promised myself I would never let anyone make me feel lesser than.

This is why this book is so important! Not only does it give me great pride and honor to be introducing this book to the world, but it gives me immense pleasure to call the author Jonathan P. Higgins, Ed.D. A doctor! My heart is bursting with joy to see how far this individual has come. To the village that raised them and to the shady gays who helped mold and shape them, thank you!

Here's why pressure makes diamonds, baby, and I have the tremendous honor of writing this foreword for this gem of a human. This book will save lives, no doubt!

Enjoy!

—Latrice Royale
Reality television personality and drag performer
September 2024

Introduction: Black, Fat, and Different

"Life for me ain't no crystal stair."

—Langston Hughes

I can remember vividly the first time someone questioned my mom about my presentation. We were sitting in a car. It was a hot summer SoCal day, and me, my little brother, and my cousins were all sitting in the back of my uncle's van. It was the early '90s, and Karyn White's "Superwoman" was blasting from the radio. I sang every last note like someone ready to go file for divorce.

"Why do you always sing girl songs?" one of my cousins turned to me and asked. I didn't respond – not because I didn't know what to say but because I knew what my cousin was inferring by asking.

Many of the questions people asked me as a child – looking back on them now – were subtle yet huge reminders I wasn't shaping up to be the man my family expected. It was also a reminder that my performance as a boy would forever be something people questioned and challenged because "boys aren't supposed to do that."

But it wasn't just the ways I sang that were challenged. Family and friends of my mother constantly asked why it seemed I always wanted to be around other girls and older women. I was constantly asked why I never had any male friends or why I never played outside with my brother and boy cousins. The truth was I never felt safe around them. As a young Black boy who didn't perform masculinity, I honestly never felt safe.

Like most queer kids, feeling safe in any environment was a luxury, and I learned very early in my life that being Black, fat, and effeminate meant I would spend a large portion of my life fighting (and yes, I mean physically too). Mentally, I was always trying to find a place where I could celebrate being myself, but those spaces were few and far between.

As a child of a single mother, I realized early on in life she would be the one to take a large brunt of the backlash for how I performed. I can recall moments of my mother arguing with my birth father about how I was being raised because he didn't like the person I was becoming. I can also recall moments my mother told me I could stay home instead of going to my uncle's place. She knew why my uncle wanted me around him: he didn't like my performance as a young boy and was going to do whatever he could to "man me up" – whatever the hell that meant.

Yes, from a young age I always knew I wasn't living up to the expectations of masculinity, and for that, the world was always going to isolate me for wanting to opt out. This would lead to so many traumatic things happening in my life that would take me so much time to heal and resolve.

Truth is, I have always known I am everything the world hates: Black, fat, and queer.

In retrospect, this made me the perfect target to be bullied. Recalling the memories I had tucked far away in the back of my brain while outlining the chapters for this book, I realized I have always known that the world carried a certain disdain for me. In reality, there has never been a time in my life where I haven't been made to feel "othered" or have been made to feel like I truly had a place in the world. Whether it was being called

2

a "nigger" by my Latinx next-door neighbors or being called "fat" by a PE instructor because I never had the endurance to run and finish the 2-mile challenge, there was always some form or epithet or microaggression looming around me, reminding me I would never be accepted without pause.

Strolling down memory lane, it's not hard for me to remember that the world didn't like me, the intersections of my identity, or the ways in which I did (or didn't) perform. My whole life has been one constant reminder that I wasn't "like other Black men" and that choosing not to conform would often make me the perfect target for hatred and oppression.

Like any other Black queer, my story begins with what I like to call "the eye." You know that look an adult gives you when you don't perform to their liking?

Yeah, that eye.

I know I have always had that "eye" on me, but it's only now that I truly couldn't care less about what said eye means. Most days I felt like even as a young child I was expected to present and act as an adult, which later in my years I learned was connected to the adultification of Black children. Meaning, society forms a racial bias of children, specifically Black children, who are treated as adults before they actually are.

I remember hearing often that I needed to "act like a man" or that I needed to be the "man of the house" because my father never wanted anything to do with me. Any moment when I didn't perform as such, there was always someone close enough to make sure I didn't step out of line or get too comfortable in my skin. And there is a certain kind of guilt that comes with this notion that you aren't performing in the ways society wants you to, especially when you are a child who has been taught to please people and seek affirmation and validation.

Throughout my earlier years, so many people said I was "cold" or "mean" because of the way I interacted with the world. I once had a teacher ask me in middle school why it always seemed that I was on guard or "ready to fight." Truth be told, it's because I was; I knew that if I didn't fight for me, no one else would. But also, it's because most of my life I spent my days doing exactly that. Whether it was me having to fight my way out of my fifth-grade bathroom because another boy thought I was looking at him as we went to pee or having to fight with my father because he didn't like that I had a pink CD case, I spent the majority of my life feeling like a mouse trapped inside of a cage with someone constantly poking and prodding at me.

As a kid, I spent my early years being angry at the cards God gave me, begging either for him to make it easier or for him to bring me home. I was good with either option. I was lonely, sad, and pissed. I was handed cards I didn't want, but more, I was mad at the world for making fun of me for having said cards. More than anything, I spent most of my life and continue to spend it questioning why the world was lax about the hatred I received. The thing that really gets me is how adults were often so much more cruel and meaner to me than my peers.

While I have been super intentional about not bonding in my trauma (or reliving it) while writing this book, there are several stories and moments I feel I need to share for you to understand why I spent so much of my youth feeling isolated and alone. Memories like being called a "fag" by one of my teachers (seventh grade, fourth period; I will never forget that day) or being told everything I will do in life is going to fail because I chose my identity over a religion. Yes, honey, I got stories for days.

I'm sure many of you have stories like this too, and if you don't have these stories, you probably know someone who does.

"Why me?" was something that played over and over in my head and only grew louder when I got to college. Not just because college is a lonely and scary time for most people, but because that is where I truly began to understand how truly messed up the world is to Black Fat Femmes.

The Internet taught me quickly that just like my childhood, there would be a lot of people judging me for how I looked and for how I performed masculinity. This came in the form of "No Black, No Fat, No Femmes" (short for feminine) on someone's dating profile. It was 2003, I was in college, and the now defunct website Gay.com was a popular place for queer men to chat.

But it wasn't just in their profiles. Chatting back and forth with men in my local area, I would send what I thought was my most masculine presenting photo, and immediately I would be blocked. Time and time again this happened, and as I was developing my own sense of self, I kept asking myself, "What is so wrong with me that men keep blocking me after I share my photo?"

On blogs and MySpace I would constantly write about it. As a feminist theory minor, I would constantly write about it in class assignments. I got deemed "divisive" in my program because I wouldn't shut up about it. I knew there was a problem, and I was 100% sure that it wasn't me.

Over time I would come to understand that there were long-standing issues of racism, fatphobia, and femmephobia that lived in the Lesbian, Gay, Bisexual, Transgender, Queer (LGBTQ+) community.

What made this so hard to process was all the phobias that lived around being Black, fat, and feminine. These were the things I learned about in my feminism course. These were all things Audre Lorde wrote about and things that Marsha P. Johnson and Sylvia Rivera had marched about. The world had nothing for Black Fat Femmes, and this is where the residual self-hatred that began to harvest in my heart and mind began to spiral out of control.

The thing was, I knew nothing about the idea of intersectionality and didn't fully understand the magnitude of the oppression I was facing, or the oppression that I had been facing. Moreover, social media was watering the self-hatred that was growing in me because I kept getting messages (literal and not) about how I needed to "act like a man" to be loved and accepted in this world. This led me to doing anything and everything I could to be masculine, because I not only wanted the approval from my family but now the approval of my suitors. It almost became a game of how long I could be myself until someone I met told me that I was too fat or too feminine.

At one point, I even stopped wearing my colored contacts because I thought they were too feminine. Regardless, no matter what I did, it seemed like there was nothing that I could do to have someone find interest in me. I was always too Black, too fat, or too femme.

While coming to terms with the fact that those in my own community weren't a fan of my intersectional identities, I found myself reverting back to the sad, lonely, and angry little boy I thought I had left behind when I got to college. After those experiences, tied with the experiences I was having in college with the men I met both online and at local queer bars, I began to internalize the hatred that society had for me while also negotiating the hatred my own community had for me.

Over the years, I would have so much work to do regarding how to unlearn that self-hate that I had taken on. I knew first hand that the world wasn't kind to Black people and fat people, and I also knew the world hated queer people. I was all three. Years later, after spending countless hours in therapy and after speaking about wanting to write a book, a light went off about what I wanted to write and why.

■ ■ ■

The thought of this book began after having what I believe was one of the most intense sessions I had ever had with my therapist. (I am sure I still owe my therapist two boxes of Puffs tissue.) After spending almost a year unpacking all the hurt and trauma I had experienced in my life and fully understanding why I hated myself, I was finally starting to connect the dots around the work I needed to do to fully like and love who I am.

My therapist asked me to write down all of the things I liked about myself and all the things I wanted to love about myself. She then proceeded to ask me to name who influenced those aspects of myself, and the names of other Black Fat Femmes kept coming up: André Leon Talley, Latrice Royale, Mayhem Miller, Dexter Mayfield, and so many more. I had dedicated my dissertation to James Baldwin and Bayard Rustin, but I had never been challenged to think about other folks who looked or lived like me and how they inspired me. The list of names began to pour out, and as I began to reflect on them, I realized that many of names were Black Fat Femme media figures who used their platforms to tell other Black Fat Femmes to love themselves unapologetically.

Moreover, these were people who showed me how to play the cards that life had dealt me.

At that moment – writing down their names, both past and present – I was beginning to outline something special. I was beginning to create a document that pointed to those in the media who were blazing a trail of self-love. I was beginning to write about why I wanted to be like many of those names I had listed on that paper, specifically because rarely does anyone talk about how important their visibility is.

Now, being someone who has begun forking a road for themselves in the media, I felt it was time to highlight how those individuals helped shape my love of self, because it is more than just simply saying "I like/love me." Being someone who is often tapped to talk about the experiences of Black Fat Femmes, I felt it was important for folks to understand how we aren't given the liberty to speak our truth when it comes to *our* experience. Black Fat Femmes are made to feel like we are a problem for speaking truth about the ways we are marginalized in a marginalized group.

I wanted to make sure that they, like you, could read about their impact and why the topic of visibility is so important.

If I had a dollar for every time someone asked me "How have you come to love who you are in entirety as a Black, fat, queer, feminine, nonbinary man?" I'd honestly be richer than Beyoncé and Jay-Z combined. While I am never shocked by the question, I do find it a bit tricky to respond to because there is no single answer that explains how much time, energy, and effort (and cash) goes into loving yourself as a Black Fat Femme.

Like anyone in the LGBTQ+ community, the hardest part of being happy with who you are is letting go of the internalized fear that follows you day in and day out. It's about letting go of all the expectations from your peers, friends, and family and creating a world around you that allows you to love everything

8

about who you are. It's also about getting over the racism, fat-phobia, and femmephobia you experience both in and out of the community.

Without a shadow of a doubt, when I talk about my journey to self-discovery and self-love, I can't talk about it without discussing the roles that television and film has played in my life, because I found so much of myself through the media. Additionally, my love for media is so much more complex than "just liking to watch TV."

I was looking for folks who looked like me on television because I didn't have access to them in my real life. I didn't know anyone who looked like me or celebrated being like me.

Much of this book is truly a reflection of how I found myself through the media. As a latchkey kid who spent most of their time being raised by television, there were moments where I would see little bits of myself in the smile, laugh, walk, and talk of a character or a guest judge on "America's Next Top Model."

I would get really close to the television with my Hot Pocket and my Shasta soda and think to myself, "I want to be as confident as them when I get older." Looking at them, they offered the lesson plan I would need to become who I am now. In so many words, the existence of Black Fat Femmes in the media reminded me that I am everything the world hates and that if I was going to make it in this world, I had to find some kind of way to love each of my identities boldly.

I would have to continue moving throughout the world both relentlessly and fearlessly and knowing that I had people, both alive and not, championing my existence because they too knew what it was like to be treated as the other.

In reflecting on why I am centering so many of these names in my book and in the story of my journey, I realize that for my first book, this is a great way for me to thank them. That

9

this book is not just about me or my experiences as a Black Fat Femme but about the ways the media plays an intricate role in helping marginalized people find community.

Over time, speaking with other Black Fat Femmes, I noted that many of them felt the same way. As I began crafting this book, I had heard so many stories of pain like my own that I began to wonder what a story of relentlessness and joy would look like and who are the ones who inspired it.

On social media, while I often talk about how interesting it is to be a Black Fat Femme as it is both complicated and beautiful, I want to spend more time talking about how we get to and stay in that beautiful place. I want others to read this and draw from those, famous or not, who inspire them to be the best version of themselves.

I think this is why I am so vocal about representation and exposure in much of my work. While I did not grow up in a small, rural part of America, there are thousands of Black Fat Femmes who have that experience so much more than I will ever be able to comprehend. Knowing this, this isn't a book to tell other Black Fat Femmes (or anyone for that matter) that "life will get better" because sometimes it doesn't. But you learn how to cope by taking the lemons life gave you and using them to make pie.

I want this book to serve as a reminder to us that we are what makes the world better and that there is so much to garner from seeing and watching us thrive.

If there was anything I truly learned from watching folks like André Leon Talley, Miss J, Latrice Royale, and so many more who will be named throughout this book, it's that their tenacity and audacity to love themselves is what gives me the audacity to love myself in a world that tells me daily that I shouldn't.

I should say, I found it extremely important for me to mention the word *audacity* at the top because that is truly what this whole book is about: how I found the audacity to love every part of me in a world that tried to tell me differently. Hell, I had to have the audacity to even pitch the idea of this book because so many people told me that it would never go anywhere.

In all honesty, one of my favorite words is *audacity* because it encompasses what it means to be a Black Fat Femme so well. By definition the word is defined as being someone who takes bold risks, specifically being brave and courageous. It's understanding that when you speak up about oppression, you will face backlash. It's understanding that to be Black in this world means being brave enough to speak up about injustice. It's understanding that to be fat means being brave enough to take up space in a world that often doesn't create spaces for you. It's understanding how the world will do its best to force you to embrace the binary but making the cognitive choice to step outside of the norm. It's about having the fearlessness to say "I'm a bad B*tch and I know it."

■ ■ ■

This book comes from a place of longing and how I found myself in a time where self-discovery wasn't something that was openly talked about.

However, at the core of this book I will get into a deeper conversation about the struggles that Black Fat Femmes deal with (or have dealt with) when trying to overcome the obstacles of both life and career and what we can learn from it. The hope is that by the end of the book, I can provide a sense of understanding as to not only who I am but how I became who I am and why that means so much to me.

While I know that much of this book will be rooted in me giving flowers to the folks who helped me see me in the media, this book will also offer up ways for us to begin actively undoing the racism, fatphobia, and femmephobia that lives in the LGBTQ+ community. It will also center the importance of us remaining visibly queer both in media and in life while offering up a true understanding of why we need to keep taking up space in a world that was never meant for us to be seen.

This book is more than just commentary on Black Fat Femmes in the media and the impact they have had on the world. Rarely does anyone in the media talk about what Black Fat Femmes have had to endure in order to get to a place where they can openly and honestly celebrate who they are.

Let the media tell it, and you just wake up one day, put on some heels and makeup, and VH1 and *World of Wonder* come knocking on your door. But if you sit down and really talk to a Black Fat Femme, you will quickly learn the importance of visibility and how – more often than not – Black Fat Femmes find love for themselves through seeing other Black Fat Femmes thriving.

That in itself is the sole focus of this book: how I found love for myself by watching and examining the lives of other famous Black Fat Femmes at a time in my life when it felt like nothing about me mattered. It's about how so many of the people in this book gave me a purpose to not just live, but to thrive.

But it's not just that – this book centers why we need more stories about Black Fat Femme people, both famous and not in the media. Our stories deserve to be told. We deserve to exist beyond the stereotypes and archetypes that are created around us.

The hardest part about preparing to write this book was that there is very little media that celebrates Black Fat Femmes.

Yes, while we are currently on a wave where we are seeing more Black Fat Femme creators on social media apps and on competition shows, there still isn't a plethora of media that celebrates us or our stories.

Rarely are we given the platform to say "I am more than my struggle." Rarely are we given the space to discuss how being a Black Fat Femme – regardless of how complicated it might be – is what in fact makes us amazing. If anything, this book is a love letter to all the Black Fat Femmes who have come before me, those who walk beside me, and those who look up to me for the relentless work I continue to do to make media more inclusive.

The content of this book was finalized after years of me going back and forth about what my first book was going to be about. I knew I wanted to write something that not only had meaning but could serve as a thank-you to all of those who continue to show up, bona fide, even in moments where they might be afraid or might be the only one taking up space in a room.

I also wanted to center the work of Kimberlé Crenshaw and her coining the term *intersectionality*, the framework I used in my dissertation to explain the ways that marginalized groups' political identities result in unique combinations of discrimination and privilege. Or – lack there-of.

My hope is that by the end of the book, you can learn something from all the work I have done to unlearn the things I was taught to hate about myself. My other wish is that when you finish this book, you will be able to not only celebrate those who laid the foundation but be able to pour into others who so often feel like they are alone in their journey.

While it would be easy for me to spend this entire book harping on how awful it is to be me and to skip over all the mess to save myself from being triggered, I want people to read this book and know that our ancestors, both alive and not, have left us with the instructions on how to stunt in this world.

In full disclosure, while I am writing this book for other Black Fat Femmes who have struggled to see the beauty in who they are, I am also writing this as a guide for my younger self. No one openly discusses how hard it is to love yourself as a Black Fat Femme.

No one talks openly about how hard it is to love yourself as a Black, fat person in a world that doesn't think that you have the right to exist or even be seen. Often so much of our insecurities come from others' lack of understanding of who we are and what we have been through. The hatred we have for ourselves isn't our cross to bear.

You know, it's that ugly thing called *projection*.

No one has yet to outline what it takes to love yourself in a world that doesn't see the humanity in your existence. No one told me how hard I would have to fight to love myself as a Black Fat Femme. No one talks about the audacity it takes to live boldly as a Black Fat Femme. Until now.

I have made it my life's work to prove that there can be so much joy in relearning to love the identities the world has tried to get me to hate and hope this book can inspire you to do the same.

Chapter 1

Always Too Much

"You're trying to zero in on something that you are never ever gonna get. . . .Look at you, just circling the airport. You ain't never gonna land."

—Luther Vandross

I distinctly remember the time in my life where I realized I could sing. I would often hear one of my uncles vocalizing, and often I would mock or imitate him because I too realized I could hold a note. However, in time I would be reminded by both family and friends in school that both my speaking voice and my singing voice weren't like other boys'.

"Why do you always sound like a girl?"

A constant thing that people would ask me and a constant reminder that my voice was "soft." While this led to me being super self-conscious about both my speaking and my singing voice, I always remember the time in school that I sang in front of the class and one of my teachers said, "You sound like a young Luther Vandross." I was giddy because I saw how my family responded to his music.

Being called a "young Luther Vandross" was a big deal for me because I knew my mother (and family) would always play Luther Vandross. Hell, my uncle sang "Here and Now" at my sister's wedding. Luther Vandross was and still is a big part of some of my core memories. In the words of my mother, "Luther Vandross could SANG!"

Not just sing but SANG.

I ran home and told my mother. I distinctly remember her just hugging me and smiling. She never really said much about the moment after that, but I can always remember the slight silence my mother carried around that moment when I told others that I could "sing like Luther Vandross" and how the world responded to me when I mentioned Luther being my all-time favorite singer.

Now, for the sake of this chapter – I have to say that before I go into unpacking that moment and the importance that Luther Ronzoni Vandross Jr. has in my story – this chapter is not about whether Luther was queer. So much of what I will be discussing going forward is around the ways the world treated me like they did Luther, specifically the speculation around his sexuality and the impact that it had on his mental health. I also want to mention that this chapter does discuss his food addiction and how I believe that so much of that was fueled by the speculation around his sexuality.

Alas, being told that I was a "young Luther Vandross" was such an important moment for me – all because for years I didn't actually believe I could sing. That event ties into a pivotal moment in my life where I can remember begging my mother to take me to one of my uncle's house parties and later learning the truth about why I wasn't able to come.

Said uncle didn't want me there because, you guessed it: "I sang and acted too much like a girl."

This was a running monologue in my head as a child, so being told by anyone that I emulated someone who I thought was "masculine" filled me with so much joy and hope. Sad, but true.

16

This led me to memorizing almost all of his catalog, not because all of Luther's music resonated with me but because I just finally felt safe enough to sing his songs without fear of being criticized for my presentation.

The thing that was hard to negotiate around my love for Luther Vandross was the joy that he brought me and how people responded to him outside of his music. As a child, I always felt like there was something so beautiful about the way he presented and carried himself in interviews. When he performed, it was as if he was so sure about the words leaving his mouth, but more, it was the way he commanded a stage that always stuck out to me.

I can remember a moment where my mother and uncle were talking about going to see him and En Vogue in concert and my mom referring to the show as "fabulous." When my aunt asked about the show, my mother indulged in the idea that Luther at moments "threw glitter" and was "really effeminate" in his presentation.

What my mother and uncle were both doing was what I had seen so many people in the media do to Luther during his time alive. Insinuate his sexuality and gesture to the idea that many of the songs that he sang were code for his love of men, and this signaled to me that being called a "young Luther Vandross" meant that I too loved men.

But it wasn't just my mother who was insinuating Luther's sexuality. I heard it on TV and on the radio. Snarky jokes from Wendy Williams and other radio hosts who felt like joking about his sexuality made for great content. I even once heard one of my teachers – yes, a teacher – make a comment that Luther's music was about his love for men and how they wish he would "just say that."

What was so interesting about this time in my life was that I was watching how my family not only treated me, but how they talked about celebrities too when it came to their sexuality.

"You know, he's a little funny" is something I heard my uncles say often, specifically referencing Luther Vandross and other Black effeminate men. "Fruity" and "sweet" were other words that I would hear them use too, words that they would throw around to describe the uncertainty they had around Luther's sexuality.

I often wondered as I got older, "What if he was?" What if Luther did come out to the world and celebrate every part of himself, without leaving so much to the world to hypothesize around?

This left me not only terrified but scared that somehow the world had figured me out.

■ ■ ■

There's no way I can talk about my experience as a Black Fat Femme without talking about religion and the anxiety it caused me. It's I think partly why my family – specifically my uncles – wanted to limit how much time I spent engaging the media.

Growing up a Jehovah's Witness (JW) meant that everything you did had to align with the organization. From television to music interest, anything that was considered secular meant it could cause you to stumble, meaning leave the organization.

The hardest part of being in the organization was feeling like everything I did, every move I made, was watched meticulously. If I spent too much time with the Sisters (the young women in the organization), I was being conditioned to be queer. If I spent too much time with the Brothers (the young men in the organization), I would somehow influence them to become queer/gay too.

At no time in the organization did I ever feel like I could exist without question. Because both sides of my family were Jehovah's Witnesses, I never got a relief from the organization. The challenge was always feeling like I had to pretend to be someone I wasn't – e.g. straight and overtly masculine.

The speculations around my sexuality caused my anxiety to come out in so many gross ways, from overeating to making elaborate plans of how to escape the organization. Often it was through unaliving myself. I often felt that dying would be a better solution than staying in a religion that never truly wanted me in it.

It's important for me to mention religion in this chapter (and this book) because so much of the unlearning self-hatred I had for both my younger and teenage self started with religion. There wasn't a moment or time in my life where I ever felt like I could be my authentic self, and often a lot of that was because I was being groomed to be the "gold star" JW that both my parents and my grandparents wanted me to be.

However, that dream for them began to fall apart as I got older, as both my family and the powers that be in the organization began to hint at knowing I was queer. At one point an elder (the men who run their congregations) pulled me to the side and told me that he was watching me to make sure I wasn't going to cause other young men in the organization to stumble.

What that moment signifies is that he and everyone who had power in that organization were doing everything in their power to keep me afraid of actualizing my identity. The sad part was that my family played into this as well and treated me in the same manner, leaving me to always feel like I was somehow on trial for something I had no control over. My sister would intentionally ask me my thoughts on Lesbian, Gay,

Bisexual, Transgender, Queer (LGBTQ+) people and then talk poorly about them, I assume to try to instill fear. Family members made terrible statements about being queer, and folks in the religion spent a lot time in the early '90s preaching against homosexuality, noting that having HIV or AIDS was God's way of dealing with LGBTQ+ people. They acted like being queer was some sort of death sentence.

It was like me liking Luther Vandross or wanting to be anything like him would be me admitting that I too was hiding a secret (which I was because I was so afraid). However, it's important to note that I was also very aware that the world was doing the same thing to Luther Vandross, and it taught me very early on how to protect myself in moments where I felt like my identity was under attack.

While religion and my parents were telling me what I could and couldn't watch, I was grateful to be a latchkey kid because being at home alone often meant I could tune into things I wanted to without the fear of being chastised for what I was watching. So, the moments I could catch Luther on MTV or on Oprah was a good day, because I wasn't just watching Luther; I was studying him. Watching Luther interviews in my younger years gave me the lexicon to be able to duck and dodge questions about my own sexuality and performance.

The hard part of watching him though was the longing for peace I saw in his eyes. How guarded he was, and how even though I didn't understand what it felt like to be in the public eye, I knew exactly what he was going through.

I would watch the ways in which he would change the subject when people asked him outrightly if he was queer. I would watch him keep his composure around topics that, even as a child, made me really angry. While I was happy that I had Luther to examine in my younger years, I was filled with so much rage over the ways I felt like I could never afford the opportunity to just exist.

For most of my childhood, I carried a heavy, sinking feeling in my stomach whenever I would meet people. I would anticipate the moment that people felt comfortable enough around me to ask the question "Are you gay?" or wait for the moment that someone else – yes, even JWs – would ask me about something I honestly didn't even have the whole answer to.

I liken the feeling of people interrogating your sexuality to that feeling of being in trouble for something you didn't do. You know that moment in your life where your sibling does something and won't admit to doing it and you both end up on punishment?

Yeah, that feeling.

For most of my childhood, and even parts of my teenage years, I walked around with this pit of fear in my stomach because I was worried that the world knew something about me, even though I never had any idea what that thing was. Most of the time, that feeling came up when I was in community with other Jehovah's Witnesses who too watched everything I said and did. I can recall countless times where certain authority figures would tell their children, specifically their male children, to be "careful around me," and still to this day, I have no idea what that meant. What I can say is that I do know that they were inferring that I was some type of deviant because of something I had no control over, and that is still something I am working through via therapy to this day.

But when I think about my own experience and think about what I saw the world do to Luther Vandross, it honestly makes sense why he seemed so defensive in a lot of his interviews. I think about one specific interview where you can clearly see Luther get very agitated when the interviewers ask him about his personal/dating life – as if the interviewer had a "aha, got him" moment. While Luther handled the moment with such grace and poise, it's something that so many queer people have to navigate.

Moreover, it made me wonder what it was like for him to feel like no matter what good he did in the world, it was going to be overshadowed by the looming question of his sexuality. It was the same feeling I carried with me for years, almost to my own detriment.

■ ■ ■

I can remember being on the playground in third grade, skipping around with who I considered to be my first best friend – for the sake of this book, we will call him Thomas. Thomas and I were so close that when he got moved to another seat in the classroom, I cried. I didn't know it then, but I was emotionally attracted to Thomas, and even now I can remember the feeling that he gave me when he held my hand.

For weeks, people questioned why Thomas and I held hands. I didn't know I "liked" him at that moment; I just remember that every time we held hands, I felt safe. However, a few days later, I tried to hold Thomas's hand while we were playing double Dutch, and he snatched his hand away.

"How come you hold hands? Boys aren't supposed to do that!" someone yelled from the other side of the playground. It was then that I realized that the world already had told me what I could and couldn't do – and how much time the world would spend speculating around my sexuality.

For years, I remembered that moment – the first time someone had come up to me and Thomas and asked us if we were gay, questioning why we sat next to each other, why we played with dolls, and why we both wanted to wear the same color most days.

How, at such a young age, do children have the under-standing to ask such a question? you ask.

The binary.

Society is fixated on identity and often believes that you – yes, you, the reader, owe everyone an explanation for how you show up. While this is something that others learn later in life, I learned it by the time I was seven. People wanted an explanation for why Thomas and I were so "different." People, including adults, wanted to understand why two young men were so attached. By the time I was old enough to tie my own shoes, I knew that I'd spend half my life not only trying to hide who I was but over-explaining the parts of me that didn't look masculine.

In January 2024, I got the honor to head down to Sundance to talk with Dawn Porter, the director of Luther's documentary, *Luther: Never Too Much*. I didn't know then that Luther's life would mirror so much of my own, specifically in the ways that the media talked about him and assumed parts of his life and identity.

What stuck out to me in watching the documentary were the ways in which people talked around Luther, but never talked *to* Luther. This is something that I remember feeling often in my earlier years, like always being the fly on the wall and knowing people are discussing you without really actualizing you.

I will never forget the scene toward the end of the film where someone is interviewing Luther and won't let up about how Luther identifies. Luther calmly expresses that he has no interest in talking about it, but the interviewer doubles down on the conversation. You can clearly see the pain written all over Luther's face, a pain that many Black Fat Femmes know all too well.

The pain of dealing with someone assuming they have the right – the privilege really – to be part of something that for so many is often so very personal and sometimes troubling.

Having to explain your gender identity to a complete stranger – someone who has no investment in your well-being – is one of the most degrading things. It's almost like someone chips away at pieces of your soul every time they ask you. And that's why it's not lost on me that toward the end of Luther's life, you could see the pain in his eyes. Because no matter how talented you are, no matter how many life-changing things you do, and no matter how many times you make other people feel good, you somehow have to over-explain your existence.

Luther was tired of it.

But what gags me most is how the world – people who have never had any interest in parts of your well-being – believe deeply in their hearts that they have a right to know the most intimate, and often most sensitive, parts of you.

Ask anyone who has grappled with elements of their sexuality: discussing it is not only draining but sometimes degrading. In most of these conversations, folks are rarely asking to fully know and understand you. They are usually asking because they want something juicy or salacious. They want to know that they have something to talk about around the dinner table.

No one knew Luther. No one had insights on how the topic might affect him or how it might trigger memories that he might not have wanted to revisit. I remember watching Luther, his body movements, and the way he folded his body into the chair. I leaned into the television, knowing exactly what Luther was feeling (and how my family was going to respond at the end of the interview). The person asking him these questions was somehow telling him to "validate his manhood" or, in some other way, to tell the world that everything they thought about him was true.

No one knew what trials and tribulations he had gone through to have the platform he had, and more, based on what I could see and remember, no one *deserved* his truth. In most cases, there is a sense of trust that must be earned around someone sharing parts of their identity, and judging from what I could see, Luther never trusted anyone with his truth.

Seeing the way the world treated him is what I believe played a great role as to why he is not here with us today.

I can remember clearly being really young when *The Kings of Comedy* came out. Again, being a JW, I wasn't supposed to be watching it, but being the rebel child I was, I watched it anyway. I will never forget one of the jokes Cedric the Entertainer included in his act about Luther, and even though it was small, it had a big impact on me.

"I like Luther," Cedric jokes. "Not little Luther, though. Big Luther."

Most of my life, I remember Luther's weight being a punchline. While there were interviews that I had seen over the years talking about Luther's yo-yoing weight, no one had ever dived into what was actually going on with Luther with care in the ways Porter did in her documentary.

In the documentary, several celebrities who were close to him note that food was Luther's safe place, and that was something I not only felt but totally understood.

It wasn't until I started outlining this book that I understood how much the early struggles with my sexuality drove my love of food and how so much of my identity was wrapped up in body politics. Something I had to unpack was that, in my mind, food was the thing that made me feel safe as a kid. Food didn't have any expectations of me. Food didn't always need me to over-explain myself, and it most certainly didn't make fun of me.

Food was my safe haven. Food, *especially* desserts, brought me the joy that so many people in my life were invested in taking away from me.

Like Luther, my weight would fluctuate often as a kid, because of getting subtle messages that being Fat *and* Femme would make me that much more of a target in school. At one point, I remember gaining close to 20 pounds in a month and being upset that all the clothes I liked wearing didn't fit.

But it wasn't just me noticing. My peers noticed it too. I will never forget the time that someone said that they didn't want me on their team while playing kickball because I was "slow and weird." I knew what the other kids were inferring: I was too fat and too queer to play with the other kids.

For weeks, I would find every reason in the book to sit out of PE because I didn't want to get picked last. I didn't want people making fun of me while I was trying to run, and I didn't want to see the other kids disapprove of me being on their team.

And let's not even begin to talk about the ways I began sneak dieting because of the jokes family members would make about my size. At one point, I asked my mom about starting Jenny Craig because kids in my class would say I needed it.

But it wasn't just the kids in my class. It was the *Arsenio Hall Show* making jokes about Luther. It was Jay Leno. It was BET's *Comic View*. I began to see and understand that Luther Vandross was in fact a punching bag not just because people thought he was fat but because people thought he was gay.

The ironic thing about it is no matter how much I would hate myself for how big I was getting, it never made me want to stop eating. In all honesty, the depression I had around the thought that no one loved me because of being queer only made me want to eat more. Add in the food insecurity I had as a child coupled by the looming fear of being judged for being queer and you have the perfect recipe for me being overweight.

Much like Luther, I assume that being bigger in some sick and twisted way made us believe that we would be safer in our body – that the mean things/questions people asked us would hurt less. But somehow, always being the bigger person (literally and figuratively) as a Black Fat Femme somehow always makes you the punching bag.

In the doc, Porter highlights the time that Eddie Murphy cracked a joke about Luther being a "KFC-eating mutha-f**ker" and how Luther brought out a large bucket of KFC at one of his shows. While so many people applauded Luther for being able to laugh that moment off, no one stopped to think about the full impact that that moment must have had on him. Luther could never be seen for his talent, but for only being someone who "loved to eat." And that's part of the journey of being a Black Fat Femme: no matter how messed up a situation is, you somehow have to learn to laugh it off in order to survive.

Somehow you have to learn how to laugh even in moments where all you want to do is cry.

■ ■ ■

I can recall the moment that one of my uncles punched me in the shoulder out of the cold blue.

"What the hell was that for?" I shouted at the top of my lungs.

"Because you need it," my uncle said back to me. My uncles and I always had a tumultuous relationship because I think they knew I saw through them, and I think they very clearly saw me as not being who they wanted me to be.

"Jonathan talks too much," one of my uncles would often say when I came around. "Don't you know how to shut up?" I did. But I knew that being "me" was something they hated, and to spite them, I would "buck up" in order to mask the pain that many of them caused me.

One of the things I learned from watching Luther in my time growing up was how he too was good with his words. His words were sharp. He was straight to the point and very matter of fact about the things he believed, especially when it came to his music.

This was something I wanted to emulate because in my family, I knew that I would keep being hit out of the blue – whether it was with words or a literal fist – if I didn't stand up for myself. Most of my life, people knew "I had a mouth," but I also recognized early on that if I didn't speak up or advocate for myself, the entire world would have made me its punching bag, because that is often what the world feels like Black Fat Femmes deserve.

But it's both the mental and physical pain that Black Fat Femmes like me never talk openly about. The stories I have . . . the time someone broke into my PE locker and threw all of my clothes in the dirty corner. Or, all the times people would tape a piece of paper with the word "fag" on it to the back of my shirt or backpack. While I knew that these moments happened because I was an easy target, none of them ever hurt me like the ways in which my family would actively go out of their way to cause harm.

One of the distinct memories I had was having an uncle tell me that I needed to be more like my male cousins and forcing me to sign up to play soccer. When I wouldn't, he would make me walk long distances to my cousin's practices (often miles) because "I needed the exercise." The world saw me as something to despise. The world still sees me as something to despise.

It was about "showing" the men in my family that I could assimilate to the ways *they* believed Black men should be. But, even when I dim my light to protect myself, it always felt like it was never masculine enough.

It never felt natural. It always felt forced.

So much of my life I thought about the ways the world, including my family, considered me "soft" and how so much of my youth was spent with family – specifically the men – looking for any reason to whoop my behind because they thought it would "toughen me up," not realizing that it was making me close off a side of me that I never fully got to understand or even explore.

As I think about the concept of softness, I think about the ways young Black men are conditioned to perform in an aggressive manner, not because they want to but because they are forced to.

An important part of my story rests around not knowing or having a strong relationship with my birth father, leading many of my uncles and peers to believe that was the reason for me being effeminate. Comments around me were that I was "too sensitive" or too "effeminate," and somehow that could be attributed to me not having enough men in my life.

But in all actuality, it was quite the opposite.

I would see the way the men in my life treated each other and think to myself, "I never want to be like that. Ever."

However, seeing how soft and kind Luther Vandross presented himself, it drew my love and admiration for him. To me, his music and his persona stood in full contrast to toxic masculinity, or the idea that he had to placate the ideologies of what it means to be a man or feed into the stigma of being violent toward women.

His songs explored themes of love, self-reflection, and an openness – a certain level of vulnerability – that so many Black men don't get to explore. Moreover, there was an emotional expression that Luther challenged not just the world to engage but Black men to examine, and that made him a target. That makes Black Fat Femmes a problem, because, like him, they challenge the traditional notion of masculinity – specifically when we think about the ways our feelings and emotions are shared.

While rudimentary, the classic notion of "men are not supposed to be soft" or "have emotions" only fuels homonegative (the idea that being gay is wrong) and queerphobic rhetoric. Vandross embraced his sensitivity and showcased that not just in his music but in how he treated people.

This is the beauty of being a Black Fat Femme and celebrating the legacy of folks like Luther Vandross. It's knowing that even with how mean, hurtful, and cold the world has been to you, you can still offer that love to the world. In a society where masculinity often promotes aggression, dominance, and emotional detachment, Luther reminded cisgender men that the best parts of life are sticking to the tenderness, empathy, and compassion that we so effortlessly embody.

While I often reflect on the joys and learnings that Luther Vandross brought me as a child, as I began to age, I started to understand what it was that both people in my family and those in the world were doing. The thought was, if they could scare me enough not to find joy in folks like Luther Vandross, then somehow I wouldn't embrace the softness and femininity that lived in me. For outsiders, the fear of me being queer surpassed my right to be happy.

For many, the fear of me being queer meant more than me being protected from harm because the thought of me being queer meant that I somehow deserved to be mistreated. It taught me very young that much of my life would mean that I too would be treated in the same manner.

As I watched the ways that I was treated differently, it made me lash out – most often to the people I loved, but mainly toward myself. For years I would stare in the mirror and cry, asking myself why I couldn't just be "normal" like the other boys.

Was I somehow bringing this on myself?

Was it my fault that the world hated me?

Could I change and not be doing everything in my power to change?

These were all the questions I kept thinking, blaming myself for the disdain that it felt like the world had for me. Only again, I would seek refuge in singing Luther's songs because I felt like the words in his songs really spoke to me:

"In my heart there's a need to shout
Dyin', screamin', cryin' let me out
Are all those feelings that want to touch
Any love?"

I might have not fully understood the song's meaning, but I knew *exactly* what Luther felt. He just wanted someone, anyone, to love him.

And it's not to say that I didn't know or have love. I truly believe that part of what kept me here to write this book today was the love I got from my brother and my mother. However, outside of that love, there is a genuine feeling of "hurt" that comes with being a Black Fat Femme, a genuine feeling that someone has told a joke about you – a joke that you will never be in on.

For years, I learned that a big part of being a Black Fat Femme was the performance. The moments where you learn very early in your life to laugh, even when you feel like crying. To smile, even though on the inside of you you're literally one "fag" away from dying.

In that, you begin to blame yourself. You begin to think that everything that has happened to you is somehow your fault because you failed to indulge the idea of masculinity. Because I refused to "perform," much like my ancestor Luther Vandross, the world was hell-bent on making me pay.

■ ■ ■

I think one of the greatest lessons I learned from Luther Vandross was that as a Black Fat Femme, the world wanted me to be its puppet. I saw how the world and my family celebrated me when I sank into myself as a child. I also saw how the world and my family punished me when I opted to step out of the confines of masculinity too.

So much of my young heart was shaped in contrast by trying to beat the stereotypes of masculinity because I knew it never "fit" me, only to learn that the world would in fact beat me into submission if I didn't emulate it. From fights on the playground to kids throwing food and soda at me for "acting too much like a sissy," the world wanted to remind me that being "me" was, in fact, a problem. I can distinctly remember the moment I felt like one of my classmates and a few of his friends were going to "jump me" because they thought that I was staring at them in the locker room.

The hardest feeling in the world as a young child is never feeling safe. Not at school, not around extended family. Always being on guard and being exhausted from trying to live up to someone else's expectation. Now, as a fully actualized adult, I often reflect on what other Black Fat Femmes can learn by watching Luther's "performance" in the world and how so much of me watching him helped me to come to understand the intersections of my own identity.

While intentional or not, I often reflect on the expectations we put on young Black boys, specifically young Black boys who identify as Black Fat Femme. Everything becomes about the "performance" of each of your identities, specifically the world wanting you to feel that somehow the mistreatment is your own.

Watching Luther Vandross demand honor and respect from the world reminded me that I too deserve to demand respect and honor. There were moments where people would ask me about my sexuality and I would say "That's none of your business!" and skip away. Or, when my family would make fun of me for saying I only sang girl songs, I would reply, "You're just jealous that you don't know how to sing."

I began to learn from Luther that I had a right to protect and honor myself even in the moments I was scared to death.

In addition, watching Luther soar in both the music industry and in his personal being (regardless of being out to the world or not) reminded me that I got to choose who I let in to engage the softer pieces of my inner being. People didn't deserve access to all of me without truly knowing and respecting me.

For me, so much of my examination of Luther's life and relationship isn't about what the world did or didn't do to protect me as a young child, or what people didn't do to protect Luther. It's mainly about honoring that we both learned to exist and push past oppression in worlds that were never built to protect us.

So while folks were so worried about me taking a page out of Luther's book and being queer, it was Luther who in fact taught me the importance of what it means to own your individuality, especially if that individuality means not looking like the other boys in the room.

Luther reminded me that it was okay for me to be demure and soft. Being soft was something special in a world that from the time I was brought into it was hell-bent on making me a rock. But the greater lesson was how Luther taught me how to protect myself when no one else would.

That will always be the thing that I hold close about Luther. He knew the world wasn't ever going to be kind to him, so he learned how to protect the softness that he had. Do I wish I could have known more about his truth? Without a doubt. But I understood very early on in life why he never shared it with the world.

Watching Luther Vandross not only defy stereotypes but present an alternative version of masculinity is in fact what helped me begin the process of not just liking myself but learning how to love myself fully. Also, it showed me how to protect myself in a world that would have left me destined for pain.

Engaging Luther and his legacy helped me comprehend that no matter what another person might do to try to harm me, my true strength lies in the ability to connect deeply with the parts of me that the world wants me to never assume. My greatest strength is my power to withstand the ways the world pressured me to be something I never ever wanted to be.

Chapter 2

The Chiffon Chronicles

"When you're in the trenches, you're fighting a war. You're going to fight a war to win and survive. You're going to come out a victor or in defeat."

—André Leon Talley

L ife has a funny way of reminding you that you don't fit in and an even funnier way of doing it constantly. Growing up, I was often the only little boy sitting joyfully with my mother in the nail shop, playing with the plastic hands that had acrylic colorful nails glued to them, even though in my uncle's car on the way there I had a ball of anxiety in my stomach because I knew he didn't agree with me going with her.

Then there were moments – sometimes subtle and sometimes not – where I would sing and dance and catch the eye of one of my uncles who would tell me to sit down, or even not to sing at all because I was "making others uncomfortable."

But the moments that stick out most to me were the times I could hear my cousins ask my brother why I "acted like a girl." These moments for some reason often replay in my mind, because even when I was just trying to be myself, I felt the pressure to always be someone else.

So, on most days, I would take solace in television, watching shows like *Jenny Jones* or *Ricki Lake*, because I knew that if I were lucky, there would be someone like me on the show.

I do, however, recall getting in trouble once because I blurted out to my mother "I like boys too" after someone came out on TV.

Without a shadow of a doubt, television was a big part of my life – often because I never had anyone around me to help me understand the intersections of my identity. While I often spent the earlier years of my life using TV as my roadmap to understanding my identity, I always found it hard to exist once it was time to go out into the world.

Even when I did watch television, I recognized the disparity that came with being "different." On television or not, I've always comprehended that both boys and girls had certain expectations and roles to play and what the consequences would be if I didn't follow them. I remember watching people on *Jerry Springer* get so angry when Black men came out as queer, wondering why the world felt the need to respond that way.

As I got older and became more versed in my experience, I began to understand that specifically Black men were expected to perform in a certain way – whether on the screen or not – and by not doing so, the world would chastise me for it.

Often, my consequence for not showing up as the "traditional" Black boy included being threatened by family members with physical harm. Once, hearing "I'm Every Woman" by Whitney Houston at an uncle's home, I began to sing and dance down his stairs as if I were the Goddess Whitney herself. Said uncle walked up to me, grabbed me by the arm, and told me that he would "knock my teeth out" if I ever did that again.

That moment taught me early on that there were expectations that came with being a young Black boy growing up in the hood of Compton and San Bernardino, California. It taught me the importance of "performing masculinity."

In talking about performance, there is so much to unpack. While I've spent years writing about this in the context of others' experiences in research, I had never sat with it in my own life before writing this book. Writing a book makes you face so many things – and the thing that I have struggled with the most while thinking about my upbringing is how so much of who I was as a child was based on performance.

I think the greater issue that I have worked through in the past few years is how oppression often pushes people to strive for perfection. From school to my "performance" as a Christian, I wanted to be liked by everyone. However, just being Black already offered a strike against me. Little Black boys don't get the chance to "mess up." We don't get the chance to "be ourselves," because so much of the world is telling us what we have to be before we even get a chance to fully know who we are.

Add in conversations about us being queer and not aligning with the "masculinity" that are forced upon us at a young age, and you have the perfect recipe for disaster. So much of my time in therapy has been me reflecting on this idea that even in the media young Black men are made to be seen as a "problem" just by existing. This is why so many of us hold on to the idea that a mask will protect us.

But so much more can be said about the ways in which Black young men are forced to "perform." While I was sure of my talents as a singer and dancer throughout my childhood years, I could never master the performance of the binary. This haunted me for a long time, specifically because of the ways that others treated me.

I remember going to Target with my mother and one of my uncles in the early 2000s and being so excited to purchase Britney Spear's "Baby One More Time . . ." album. Except, I wanted the pink one. The moment I went to grab it, my uncle screamed "That's for girls!" and set it back down. I grabbed the blue copy instead and walked out disheartened, wondering why everything in the world was either for boys or for girls.

More, being embarrassed as my uncle berated me for liking Britney Spears.

But that was the messaging that came from both my family and my peers that because a lot of the things I liked "was for girls." Specifically because I enjoyed listening to songs by women. To my family, that made me "soft." This would lead to me hearing my family having "nature versus nurture" conversations about me, specifically because my father was never in my life.

Often the question would come up for me of "why I didn't act like my brother" or "why I wasn't into the things that young little Black boys should be into." I never got into toy cars or toy guns or even wanted to "hang with the boys." Truth be told, masculinity has always made me very uncomfortable. In truth, it scared me.

However, so did being perceived as "soft." I knew what that meant, and I knew what people were trying to imply.

While I can go on for days about "toxic masculinity" and the impact it had on me, it is important to talk about the ways that the term *soft* impacted me more and the ways that Black Fat Femmes are often forced to be something they're not. Note that I have always been an empath – and I think that is why I got so much heat as a child.

Being "soft" – or what I like to now call being an empath – meant that I was always hyper aware of my feelings and how people made me feel. However, being "soft" in the hood meant one thing: "that nigga is a fag."

Whether I heard the F-word in my day-to-day or on TV, I would always be triggered. I knew how much my family hated queer people and hated the thought that I, a "soft" little Black boy, could possibly grow up to become one.

Even with all the therapy I have done, I have yet to fully undo all the pain that comes rushing back when I hear the word *fag*, because I knew what people were saying to me when they would call me that. While it becomes easy to shake that word off when it comes from your peers, I still struggle with the memories that I have of that word and it being used by the people I loved.

On two separate occasions I was called a fag by a family member – once by an uncle and once by my stepfather. Both of these men exemplified what many know in the world as "toxic masculinity," and I knew at a very young age that I never wanted to be like them.

In the instance with my uncle, I was called a "fag" for not wanting to participate in summer football. My uncle had signed me up for it because he believed that it would help "toughen" me up. I still to this day have no idea how my uncle rationalized using football as a way to make me less queer, but heteronormativity doesn't use logic.

The more painful moment I was called a "fag" was when my stepfather and I got into a heated argument and he knew my points were valid. I was just starting my junior year of high school, and he and my mother were going back and forth about me hanging out with my group of friends who were girls.

"That's why he's acting like a fag now" was his response, telling me exactly what he – and the world for that matter – thought about me.

Being called a "fag" was so normal to me that I learned to accept it, even though it made me viscerally angry. I can recall a bully yelling it loudly in class once after slapping me in the back of the head, and all I could see was red. All I can remember from that moment was coming into the principal's office and seeing the bully with a bloody nose, holding an ice pack to his eye.

I can't deny that as both a child and a teenager I carried a lot of rage in me. I was angry for a multitude of reasons, but mostly because I knew the world treated me differently for being different. Add in the anger I carried from having an absentee father and growing up dirt poor and you have the perfect recipe for someone who is a ticking time bomb.

This insidious thing about the rage I carried was that before I started therapy, I never knew what was going to trigger the rage. I just knew I was mad at the world for being so unkind to me and God bless anyone who caught me on a bad day.

But no matter how hard I tried to follow the advice of my uncles or other men who came in and out of my life, I never seemed to be able to perform masculinity in a way that would keep me safe. If anything, I got teased for trying to pretend to be something I clearly had no experience in – performing masculinity.

The tormenting got so bad that I began carrying a fork in my pocket because I often got chased home from school by guys (and girls) who made fun of me for being effeminate. On this specific day I knew that if anyone was going to bother me, I was ready to use said fork enough to go to juvenile hall. At this point in my life, I was ready to hurt someone, even if it was with a worn-out fork. At that moment, I wasn't thinking rationally. I just knew that I was sad and tired of being angry all the time about something someone had to say about me.

As time went on in my life, I pondered why the world had such a visceral hatred for those who were different. Even more, I wondered how people in the world knew my backstory and my upbringing and still made it difficult for me to survive.

Reflecting on it now, I understand that what people wanted from me, even at my young age, was for me to buy into the binary. That's because for most cisgender heterosexual people (people who identify with the gender they were assigned at birth, and they choose romantic partners of the opposite sex) in this world, the binary seems harmless. Many believe that the binary is just a part of who we are as a people – boys do this and girls do that, end of story. But, knowing what I know now, so much of what I went through as a child was about control and manipulation, something fed to me through religious teachings.

This begins to make things even more complex when you add religious teachings about the performance of gender with Blackness and identity politics and what it looks like to tell your Black Christian father that you don't like the idea of "being a man." This can also be dangerous when you live in gang territory and you don't "bang" (a slang term for those who are in gangs) like many of your peers.

Speaking of Christianity, do you know how messed up it is to grow up with religious ideals telling that you are going to die because of who you are? On top of trying to navigate the racism and homophobia the world puts on you?

At points, I kept thinking "Why would God do this to me?" to a point that I almost made the decision to go meet my maker and tell them to their face that this life was, in fact, too much.

■ ■ ■

Before I get into what it was like to grow up in what I now believe is a cult, I think it's important to understand how so much of the religion's teaching impacted my mental health and how it fed into my struggles around ideation (and how it shapes my ideations now). I have never spoken publicly about my thoughts on the Jehovah's Witness organization, considering that some of the folks I love and cherish are still connected to the organization and I wouldn't want to bash them for believing in something that they feel works for them.

However, the religion *never* worked for me and, if anything, only made it more complicated for me to exist. Frankly, growing up as a Jehovah's Witness and being queer was hell because there was this feeling that I never could live up to the expectations of those in the organization, as well as the expectations of my family. In addition, the religion constantly reminded me that being me (mainly queer) would lead me down a dark road of not having friends, family, or a chance to see "paradise" because I was *choosing* a certain "lifestyle."

Then came the moments of isolation because of how I presented – being deemed overly effeminate and not living up to the hypermasculine expectations that both my grandfather (who was a well-respected elder) and the men in my congregation had.

I was often scolded for how I performed – both publicly and in private – and was even told at one point that I was the reason another young boy in the congregation was "faltering in his ways" – all because of the ways I presented.

But that wasn't the half of what drove me to feel alone. We weren't allowed to have birthdays. No parties (except anniversaries). No holiday celebrations. We weren't even allowed to salute the flag (who would want to anyway, but I digress). Pretty much, I was the outcast's outcast because not only was I "odd" in the eyes of my peers in school, but I was deemed "trouble" in my congregation, all because I didn't adhere to the scope of masculinity that those in the organization wanted me to live up to.

The thing that very few people know about the religion is that there is very little time for you to engage with anything fun because the religion makes it damn near impossible for you to have a social life.

As a kid, you are pretty much in meetings almost 10 hours a week. If your parent is an active pioneer, which my mother was, I was always with her knocking on a door or engaging in some form of convention or function that the religion requires. I honestly didn't have time to think about anything else because most of my time was spent being scared that I was going to die if I displeased Jehovah (God).

So much of my life being raised as a Jehovah's Witness was me living in fear and looking for approval, whether it be from my peers, my family, or the elders (the men who are designated to "shepherd" the congregation).

But it doesn't stop there. After having a conversation with one of the elder's in the congregation because he noticed me becoming more effeminate, he made the recommendation for me to get baptized. This was not because I was passionate about the religion, but because he noted that it would help shape me into being what "Jehovah wanted." At that time in my life, I barely knew what I wanted – not just because I was young but because I had never been given the time to fully understand who I was.

I knew I was queer, and I was becoming okay with it. However, things ramped up when the brothers in the religion began to believe one of my "close friends" and I were more than friends.

To put it plainly, I was coerced into getting baptized because the elder who was "studying" the Bible with me was afraid I was going to admit I was queer. This elder thought that if I prayed hard enough and "gave my life to Jehovah," it would change something in me, and I would one day give up the "gay ghost" (his words, not mine). After getting baptized at the age of 14 and professing that I wanted to "give my life to Jehovah," I was basically expected to give every waking moment of my life to the religion.

Now looking back, the religion wanted to make me so busy that not only did I not have time to hang out with my "friend" (who was in fact my boyfriend and went to another Kingdom Hall), but I did not have time to engage the person I wanted to become – especially because so many people knew I had a love for television and film.

My life in a nutshell was nothing but school and religion. As a new "baptized" brother, the expectations were amplified, and it didn't matter how old I was, the expectations were there.

Being baptized meant:

- Preparing for each of the three meetings we had every week (about 1.5 hours of preparation a week)

- Going to said three meetings every week (Ministry, Bible Study, and Sunday Watchtower Study)

- Being in service weekly, averaging no less than 25 hours of door-to-door canvasing (you know those moments when they knock on your door – yeah, the religion tracks it)

- Studying (indoctrinating) at least two to three other people at a time

Keep in mind: I was only a teenager.

All of this in addition to the pressure I was under to stay out of trouble, hide my queerness, and be the "perfect" Jehovah's Witness had me ready to break. I was depressed and sad, but I often hid it because I knew many people in my family were happy about me being baptized and so engaged in the religion.

I am pretty sure you know where this story is going. Yep. Suicidal ideations began to take over whatever open space I had left in my brain for thoughts.

For many years, I prayed to Jehovah and asked him why he would create me only for the world to hate me. Why was I being given all these rules about who I couldn't be and who I needed to be at the same time, and why did I, out of anyone in the world, have to be the person to deal with them?

It was emotionally draining.

As I got older, I began to understand that a big part of the way I felt about my life and myself was because of the isolation that came from being raised a Jehovah's Witness. Beyond not being able to engage with people outside of school, you are limited to what you can watch or engage with when it comes to media. That means music was limited. Movies were limited. TV was limited. You name it, it was censored.

I had no one that I could trust or talk to about my experience in the religion or about being queer, and it began to wear on me. I would scour the television for any type of representation because I just didn't want to feel alone. (I didn't know then that all representation isn't good representation.)

Some days I would walk home from school, going over all the ways I could unalive myself. I would get home, turn the computer on, and Google all the ways I could do it in the least painful way – and what would happen to me when and if I did it.

I had heard on several accounts that Jehovah didn't approve of someone taking their life, but honestly, I just wanted the sadness to end more than anything. I hated being alive. I hated feeling like I was target practice, and I hated knowing that this could be the feeling I would have for the rest of my life if I decided to deny myself and stay in the organization.

The fear was deeper than I could manage because I kept looking around and thinking that this couldn't be my life for the rest of my life. The pressure was causing me to lash out at everyone because I was so angry at the world for how it was treating me. But more, the bullying was becoming more violent and persistent to the point that my mother thought it would be better for me to go live with my uncle and my three boy cousins in Moreno Valley, California "because I needed a stronger male presence in my life."

But a male presence wasn't the problem. I needed people to love me and let me be my authentic self. I needed people to let go of toxic ideologies of what a young man should be and how he should perform. I needed my family to embrace me and remind me that they loved me regardless of what the Bible or the world said about me.

That never happened, and I truly don't know how I got through that time in my life, especially all the loneliness and sadness I experienced at the beginning of my teen years.

■ ■ ■

Within the first few weeks of me living with my uncle, I fell into a deep depression. I didn't have the words for it at the time, but I knew something wasn't right. I was never off guard, and I was always worried about something.

This led me to eat around the clock. Even though I still kept thinking about unaliving myself and how I would do it, food began to replace my want to die. The joys of eating became the thing that I was more interested in because, in a weird way, food was the thing I felt connected to.

I was obsessed with the food from AMPM, a local convenience store, and having one right down the street from my uncle's house made it easy for me to both get away and to get my fix. Daily, I would save my lunch money and stack it until the end of the week. When Friday or Saturday came, I would walk down to the AMPM and eat like there was no tomorrow.

On the corner sitting alone. Eating bags of Chili Nacho Doritos and enough chili dogs to put Sonic the Hedgehog to shame.

However, the best part of living with my uncle was that he was rarely home to keep an eye on me, and when he was home, he was asleep, so no one really cared about where I was, what I was doing, and who I was doing it with. The best part was that my uncle wasn't a Jehovah's Witness, so that meant that my cousins and I could pretty much get away with anything that we wanted to without any major repercussions. Smoke weed? Sure. Try having sex? Sure.

But be queer? Absolutely not.

While there were more salacious things that *everyone* in my family got into that I never had enough nerve to do (I was still a bit more reserved and living with the fear of both the religion *and* my Black mother in me), the one thing that *not* having to engage in the religion did for me was give me more free time.

This meant I had more time after school to come home and do my homework and watch anything and everything I wanted.

Additionally, my uncle had satellites and VCRs in almost every room in his home and had every channel you could name. That gave me a chance to watch pretty much anything I wanted, whenever I wanted, including porn.

When I wasn't sneak-watching gay porn to try to understand "how it all worked," I got turned on to shows like *Undressed* and *My So Called Life*. I got so wrapped up in those shows that I began to believe that one day I would soon be able to go to college, come out, and live my best life and, that one day, all the stressors I had would be long gone.

Girl, when I tell you I was wrong, I was *big* wrong.

Thinking about it now, so much of what television told me about being queer in the late '90s and early 2000s was a bold-face lie. It didn't consider race. It didn't consider religious oppression. I never knew about the fatphobia that lived in the LGBTQ+ community, and in the world frankly. And while I was getting subtle notions that the world didn't like me, I still lived with the fantasy in my head that one day I was going to be free of all the pain and strife that surrounded me.

I believed that once I went to college and came out, I would live a life like Will Truman from *Will and Grace*. I believed in my heart of hearts that my life was going to look like the characters on *Queer as Folk* and being out would open me up to a whole community of people who loved me. The media gave me a very white-washed ideology about how my life would look after I came out.

There are things that television didn't show me as a Black queer kid growing up in the middle of San Bernardino, California. Yes, there were moments when shows hinted at the idea that college would make my life a little easier (it didn't, but we will get to that story later) – television painted a very white idea of what coming out looked like.

Television never told me that I would have so many peaks and valleys to climb to loving myself, all while navigating the hatred my family had for queer people. Television shows also never made the want to die go away either, and this was something that only progressed with time.

What's interesting to think about is all the subtle messages I got from the media about how my life, regardless of where I lived, didn't matter. What made that message even louder was that just a year before being sent to live with my uncle, the story of Matthew Shepard had hit the news and had everyone – especially my family – in a frenzy.

Matthew was a young white kid from Laramie, Wyoming, who was a victim of a senseless hate crime that ended with him losing his life. While it has come out over recent years that the death of Matthew Shepard was over something fueled by alcohol and drugs, the media had taken the story and spun it to be about Matthew's sexuality.

So without fail, being from a family that didn't have a nuanced understanding of media like they do now, I think my family overreacted, through no fault of their own, which I totally get now.

Looking back, I can understand why my mother might have sent me away even though it was only a few miles away from her. I think after hearing about a young queer boy being murdered, it kept my mother wondering if the same thing could happen to me, even though I was still very much sheltered via religion.

I was still getting beat up. I was still getting death threats slipped into my locker in middle school. I was still dealing with the ideation of suicide, and even though I wasn't outrightly acting on them, I was still giving everyone in my family pause because they knew something was wrong with me. They might not have been able to put their finger on what I was dealing with specifically, but everyone knew that I was dealing with something.

While depressed (and being told that I didn't need to talk to a doctor because I had God), I spent most of my days running home from school and doing my homework as fast as I could so that I could lock myself in my room. Though I never really had privacy as I was sharing the room with my cousins, I was still able to sit in the room and watch as much television as I wanted to.

By this time, I would spend hours, if not days, watching TV to try to get outside of myself and the sadness I carried.

Music videos were my muse, so that meant I spent most of my days watching music videos and pretending I was Britney Spears. In my mind, I had the dream that I was going to be a huge singer one day and that the world was going to embrace me in the ways that it had embraced Elton John.

While television became an escape and I was able to find some stories of being queer here and there, it also fed me with so many false hopes and lies about what my life would look like once I came out. Television never prepared me for the "after" of me coming out. The ways my family would treat me once they accepted that I was in fact queer and not everything they hoped I would aspire to be.

I still remained hopeful that one day my life would in fact turn around, all because I finally had some knowledge about what I wanted my life to be from the shows and characters I was watching day in and day out. It was a very white knowledge, but at that moment, *anything* was better than nothing.

After being asked to come back home so I could work and help my mother with the bills, I was fully thrusted back into the Jehovah's Witness organization, but this time, it was maximum speed. My mother and others in the organization believed that if I would surround myself with nothing but Jehovah's Witnesses, if I went out and ministered more and studied even more than I was already studying, it would somehow drive away my "desires" to be queer.

If anything, being further isolated in the organization only made my want to get away stronger. I was internally dying, doing anything and everything I could to figure out how to break away from the organization without losing my entire family in the process.

Black. Fat. Femme.

This led to every waking moment after my 15th birthday dreaming of what my life would look like once I "got free." I would see my peers in school, especially the queer ones, holding hands with their significant other and being "in love," wishing and hoping that it would happen to me.

I would spend hours glued to the television, immersed in the worlds of LGBTQ+ characters who (I thought) were like me, vying for freedom to be their authentic selves.

No matter how many times I got in trouble for watching *Will & Grace, Queer as Folk,* or RuPaul's show on VH1, it was a risk I was willing to take because they were the shows that made me feel a little bit better about being me. About being alive, really.

However, it was a silly little show titled *America's Next Top Model (ANTM)* that would literally offer me the lifesaver I didn't know I needed.

■ ■ ■

In hindsight, *ANTM* was awful. Thinking about the ways that Tyra Banks basically traumatized those poor contestants and how so many of those judges went right along with it?

Tragic.

However, what made the show so entertaining for me wasn't just the people on the show but how I actually watched the show. Whenever the show was on, my friends and I would three-way call each other and talk mess about each of the contestants and how insane the challenges were.

One day, after *ANTM* judge André Leon Talley made a comment, one of my friends on the line said, "That is so something Jon would say." I was caught off guard by the comment because I had never given André's critiques that much attention. But specifically, after the Yaya and Kenti hat episode in cycle 3 – yeah, you know the episode where all the white judges on the panel made fun of the Black girl for wanting to lean into her African roots and André came to her defense? – I started paying more attention to André because he embodied the person that I one day hoped to be.

Making sure I also give Ms. J her flowers too, I can't recall ever seeing queer Black people who spoke so candidly and openly about their identity. Ms. J was definitely a force to reckon with. (I talk more about them later in the book.)

But it was André who captivated me.

I began to wonder how André got to that place – the place where he didn't let racism, fatphobia, or femmephobia stop him from attaining his dreams in fashion. How did he overcome the oppressive ways society silenced Black queer people? I needed to know this man because he wasn't just a figure on my television screen. André was in fact the light at the end of my very dark tunnel.

I began going to school a little bit earlier to get to the library so that I could research André's history. I also got a chance to see the really cute boy in my class who often showed up early to do last-minute homework, so going to the library early became a win-win.

I wouldn't say that I was obsessed with André, but I talked about him a lot. In so many ways, he was a lot like me – outwardly speaking about having lived on limited means, living in really broken-down homes, and having to take "bird baths" before school. Considering that all André had was his dreams, I felt like I could see myself in parts of his struggles, specifically in struggles that he had with negotiating his race and his gender identity.

Because of André, I began gravitating openly toward fashion, working with folks in my school's fashion club and joining the creative arts club. When I was at home, I would begin thinking about how I was going to follow in his footsteps, specifically when thinking about going to college and how one day I would cross paths with him.

Beyond the accolades that André had attained – going to an Ivy League college, pulling himself out of poverty, and working with some of the influential brands and models – there was something special about seeing a Black, fat, queer man stand on the stage who spoke with such power and reassurance.

André knew that the world was waiting to slip the rug from under his feet, yet somehow he still maintained a glide when he walked. Beyond him being a champion for inclusion who broke several glass ceilings, he challenged the fashion industry to operate from a place of "unconditional love," which he said he learned as a young child from his grandmother.

What I found more interesting about his journey was that for someone who struggled so much in his past and knew that people were actively trying to ruin his future, André still moved with so much grace. More, he was the embodiment of empathy, something for years I have actively struggled with.

André also highlighted something that was major for me: not giving in to the ideology that he had to perform masculinity in a specific way for the world to receive him. At that time in my life it was the validation I needed to be able to say that one day I too could have the ability to love myself unconditionally – something that I didn't know he was offering in just being who he was.

Most days I felt like I had a dark cloud over my head, but seeing André on the red carpet of E! and on *ANTM* every week was the subtle nudge I needed to keep going. While there were moments that I was truly afraid to say out loud that he was my hero for fear of more teasing and abuse, having him in my life at that time taught me the importance of telling people that they didn't have to like me, my race, or my size, but they had to respect me. That was something I felt like I never truly deserved because of my intersectional identities.

But André's existence was more than that for me. Watching him from afar and thinking of him as I reflect on my own journey in the media, I have often felt as if I could hear him telling me to "keep my head up" on days when I felt as if I was being told to stay in my lane. He made me feel as if I belonged in this world.

He accomplished so much during his time on Earth (I mean, he was a mentor to Naomi Campbell for Christ's sake), but more than that he affirmed Black Fat Femmes. He told us that, whether it was on camera or not, we deserved the right to have joy, success, and love. He taught me I have the right to move beyond survival and the right to thrive. He reminded Black Fat Femmes that we have the right to walk with our heads up because the world is and will be nothing without us.

I would be discrediting him if the only thing that I highlighted was the way that he shook an industry built on oppression and white supremacy. Even though fashion bullies would say and do terrible things to André, he reminded us that it's not what anyone in this life calls you but what you answer to. I never knew I needed that message, but somehow – every time I saw him – that message would come through loud and clear.

André managed to sharpen his ability to make the world not only hear him but see him. André showed many how to navigate spaces, industries, and a world that was never built for them and told me that I could own it all by simply saying "I am worth it because I said so."

While his eyes were always "starved for beauty," he culti-vated a world where fat, Black, queer people like me could feel not only beautiful but important. Navigating a world in what he described as his "armor," André is and will always be of the moment.

I should say, writing this book was truly inspired by my love for him, and there isn't a time that I don't get sad that I didn't get to meet him or share with him the impact that he had on my life.

Writing about him often makes me feel emotional, not just because I looked up to him and honored everything he was but because he and his work gave me the ability to dream. Reflecting on where I am now in my life, André's existence told me that I would be able to do greater things and that Black Fat Femmes have the right to take up ALL the space. André spoke with intention and moved so fiercely, almost as if he knew the world was waiting for his demise and yet he continued to soar.

But it's not to say that André didn't get mistreated too. Many wouldn't know by looking at him that he had been ousted by his position at *Vogue* and was damn near poor in his last years here on Earth. But, André being who he was, he would prob-ably suggest that we forgive them, because we are not who people say we are but who we want to be. He may even sug-gest that there are far more important things to worry about, and thinking about our enemies won't change anything.

For me, André didn't just teach me how to love but how to embrace the journey that comes with being a Black Fat Femme. I will always remember André as the person who reminded me that it is okay for me to just be, something that no one ever gave me the agency to do. There isn't a day that I don't think about him and everything he did for me and how I will never get to tell him. If anything, I am so grateful to him because without him, I don't know where I would be or if I would still even be here to tell you this story.

■ ■ ■

Andre's lived experience mirrors so many of the issues many Black, fat, queer individuals face on the regular. Media – whether knowingly or unknowingly – often paints Black Fat Femmes who outwardly express themselves as confident as something detestable, being that we live in a grand state of delusion. I would even go as far to say the media had a macro-aggressive way of painting André as something the world should view as obscene.

As research notes, so much of what we see in the media isn't just racism or femmephobia but that of "sexual racism," stemming from the ways the media paints a portrait of what is and is not desirable in the LGBTQ+ community. Moreover, so much of what we see celebrated in the media around queerness – specifically white queerness – is that of the heterosexual archetype and how the media perpetuates this both on scripted and nonscripted shows.

But this concept of sexual racism is only a symptom of a bigger problem that Black Fat Femmes face, specifically when discussing stigma. The idea that if the media can get the world to hate Black Fat Femmes, we will fade away or disappear.

Though I should be flabbergasted about the challenges shared about his rise to fame in the '80s and the struggles he faced while working in the fashion world, saying I was would be a stone-cold lie. It's also no surprise to me why André struggled to find love. Media and the world alike has harped on the idea that to be someone who looks and lives like André means shame – shame that often keeps you being the minority within the minority.

What's more damning when looking into Andre's world is thinking about the ways he was treated for simply liking who he was. From being passed over for opportunities to being shut out of *Vogue* and left to his own devices, it's learning what other white queer folks said about him that speaks volumes. In one interview, André shared how at one point in his own career the head of PR for Yves Saint Laurent called him "Queen Kong."

Yes, you read that right. Queen. Kong.

As André expressed in his documentary, *The Gospel According to André*, it did not bother him knowing folks in the fashion industry saw him and his fullness as a threat. The doc amplifies the ways in which the media (and society) demonize Black Fat Femmes who stand in their authenticity, even when we aren't given the proper footing to stand on.

In all, examining both my own and Talley's lived experience offers insight into why we must examine the issues that Black Fat Femmes face. Beyond the ways people and media feed into racism, sizeism, and queerphobia, there is something to be said about the ways the oppressed harm the oppressed. I have experienced more oppression from others who share so many of the same intersections of identities I have, as if treating me poorly will somehow get them further in life.

However, as there is so much beauty in the struggle, we all know that there is so much we can learn from both his confidence and his elegance.

Chapter 3

The Making of a Queen

"If you can't handle the heat, get out of the kitchen."
—Jason Williams

It's interesting how much power we can give certain words in our lives and how some of them can cause such a visceral reaction. For years, I had only ever been called gay, fat, and queer, and while said words would make me cringe when other kids at school would hurl them at me, for some reason they never really got under my skin.

However, *queen*?

That was a different story.

Frankly, embracing the word has been a journey. Much like I had to embrace the word "fat," there was so much I had to unpack in order to see the word and understand the beauty of it.

Much of that journey begins with the deep-seated internal homophobia I carried. When I learned what the slang of the word meant and *who* got called queen in the LGBTQ+ community, I did anything and everything that I could to run from it. Keep in mind that because of how sheltered I was growing up a Jehovah's Witness, there were so many words I was introduced to during what I like to call my "coming-out season," words that I didn't know were almost as daunting as the words I had been called all my life by random people and folks in my family.

So let's begin with what I like to call a queer English lesson. In queer slang, "queen" is often noted as being someone who is flamboyant and highly effeminate – someone who I once heard reference me as "a person who opens their mouth and a purse falls out."

In most cases, being labeled a queen is not something that queer cisgender men would ever want to be, considering how often they are looked down upon in the LGBTQ+ community. Why are "queens" looked down upon? you ask.

Sexism.

That's right. Sexism and femmephobia is something that is rampant in the LGBTQ+ community and rarely is being any type of feminine ever celebrated. This is also why so many nonbinary and trans women – specifically Black trans women – have issues when they opt to share their experiences. A statement you will often hear from other cisgender queer men in the community is "If I wanted to date a woman, I would." This is often inferring that exhibiting any type of feminine characteristics or traits is not only unattractive but unwelcome.

Imagine being treated poorly by folks outside of the LGBTQ+ community for being effeminate and then coming out thinking you're safe to be yourself in the queer community, only to be labeled a "queen" and then experience rejection all over again.

In my case, I figured that if the world was going to chastise me for being a "queen," I would play it up. I'd be everything the world said I was: catty, mean, overly loud, and always looking to be the center of attention.

While much of me playing into the idea of being a "queen" was because I was dying for the world to "see me," a lot of it was me simply responding to the ways in which the world had always treated me. I was used to being teased, and I had become super defensive. My mind was always riddled with what others thought about me – both inside the religion and out – and what I would need to do to win their approval.

Most, if not all, of my teen years I was picked on, so yes – in my mind I believed that being "catty and mean" would keep people from hurting me when all along I was the one who was really hurting. Playing into the idea of "being a queen" was a simple way of life for me because if I was too nice or too passive, I believed that someone would read me as a queer and say (or do) something to harm me.

People would always say that I "had a way with words," but much of it was me spending a lot of time thinking about something someone could say to me and how sharp I would have to be with my comeback.

I had to protect myself, and if being a queen was the way I could do it, so be it.

I had to make sure that my response would cut like a knife, and even now I have to watch what I say because I know my words (and actions) can be really sharp. Trauma will do that to you.

But a lot of the pain in my younger years came from being compared to my mother.

"You act just like your mother!" would often be a response from my uncles and my male cousins, because my mother, too, has a strong vocabulary. My mother is sharp. Her words are witty, and when she strings a sentence together to take aim, you better run for cover.

Even at my young age, I knew what people were trying to say. Even though I didn't fully understand what sexism and femmephobia was, I knew "acting like my mother" wasn't a compliment. I always knew it meant "You're acting like a woman."

But over time I would learn to wear that statement like a badge of honor, because "being a queen" and "being like my mother" reminded me of how strong Black women are and how strong I have fought to become. Though I know Black Fat Femmes are treated like Black women, specifically in the vein of being dismissed and looked down upon, I began to understand the interesting intersection I would forever live in. I would understand what civil rights activist and scholar Kimberlé Crenshaw meant when she coined the term *intersectionality*[1] and how so much of the word's meaning would give me the meaning I had always been looking for.

■ ■ ■

I will continue to scream from the mountain tops that the media and entertainment in the early 2000s was a lie, specifically when it came to learning how to navigate the LGBTQ+ community.

Now before you go judging somebody, keep in mind that while I grew up in Southern California, my interactions with other Black Fat Femmes were far and few. Because of my religion and my own fear of being outed, I did anything and *everything* I could to stay away from anything that would deem me queer or a queen.

---

[1] The term was first used in Kimberlé Crenshaw's published article, "Demarginalizing the Intersection of Race and Sex: A Black Feminist Critique of Antidiscrimination Doctrine, Feminist Theory, and Antiracist Politics." The University of Chicago Legal Forum, issue 1, article 8 (1989).

That meant sneaking and watching queer television. That meant deleting text message threads I had in high school with friends who were talking about LGBTQ+ storylines in shows. I remember having a huge crush on one of the Backstreet Boys and being so afraid to ask my mother for tickets to the show because why would a 16-year-old Black boy want to go to a Backstreet Boys concert?

Even though others would call me "queer" and "gay," no one ever sat down and talked to me about what it actually meant to be "queer." Everything I learned about being queer I learned from TV, and much of it was about being a white queer person, honestly.

In the early 2000s, at the height of what I like to call the "coming-out revolution," most, if not *all* the "coming out" stories I saw came from white media figures. Television focused only on white queer narratives, which is why I still have so many issues with America's version of *Queer as Folk* to this day.

I was semi-familiar with the *Ellen* show and had watched the show to get an understanding of how to come out. However, shows like Maury Povich, Jenny Jones, and Ricki Lake left me terrified of how my family would react – especially after seeing how folks responded to Ellen in real time.

Being deeply immersed in pop culture, I began to trick myself into believing that my coming out would result in some type of "coming-out party" like the guys on TV where random people would embrace me and love on me, affording me the emotional freedom and weightlessness that I had always been longing for.

Television told me that going to college and coming out would mean freedom and being able to find my voice, all it would take for me to get there was shoved into a tiny little box of expectations. No one told me that the stories the media were painting of queer liberation were only for white queer kids.

However, because so much of my life was shaped by what I thought was reality, I just knew that college would be the thing that would give me the freedom I longed for. Beyond being wrapped up in my own imagination about what liberation I would find once I got into college, I was spending my days and night rewatching episodes of MTV's *Undressed*, dreaming about the things I'd finally get to do and all the boys I would finally get to date.

Because I saw so many white people being loved and accepted by their peers I thought coming out would mean the same for me. What television had failed to teach me was that these stories were fiction, and most, if not all, of my family would turn their backs on me when I came out.

I truly believed – again, because of television – that coming out would give me authority and autonomy. I saw how the world responded to Andre León Talley. I had seen how people loved and embraced the gays on *ANTM*, so I figured, "When I come out, the world will embrace me in the same way."

I thought I had my coming-out moment all figured out. Until I didn't.

With all the fear I had practically beaten into me about actualizing my identity, I knew that coming out meant risking not just my own family and the community that I had in the organization, but mainly my livelihood. I heard the ways people in my organization talked about LGBTQ+ people. I had seen the ways my family judged them. I had heard my sister make mention that they all should die.

"They should be ashamed of themselves!" I would hear my grandmother quip. "You know what Jehovah thinks about that,"

I would often hear people in my religion say to me at any moment that they thought I was being unholy.

So, I felt that the easiest way for me to keep the people who knew me off my back was by pretending that I too had issues with LGBTQ+ people while also dreaming of being able to say it publicly one day. This festered and fueled a lot of the self-hatred that I had and would shape a lot of the ways I talked about Black Fat Femmes I saw in the media – including André.

I never really got a chance to actually engage my identity outside of what I saw on television, and the hard part about only having media to help shape my identity was the mixed messaging I got about what it meant to be young, Black, fat, and queer. On one channel I had Dan Savage telling me that "It Gets Better" for LGBTQ+ people, while on another channel I was being told by Tyra Banks and Janice Dickenson that my size, skin color, and hair were a problem.

I was always left with the question of "who am I?" outside of these shows. The reality of it all was that as a youngish Black, fat, queer kid, the messaging was super ambiguous, mainly because I never had anyone to process or make sense of my identity with. Even now, I still struggle with an answer to that question.

I was beyond lost. It felt like no matter where I turned, the world was finding any kind of way to reassure me that being out and proud was not the person that I should ever want to be. However, I still kept looking for representation, even though my religion (and family) didn't support it.

Imagine being told that if you did look to another queer person in the media for strength, you would die because you were not upholding the values you were forced to have.

Sad, right?

This is when I made the decision that if I was ever going to be able to be fully myself, I needed to get away from both my family and the religion. This decision was easy to make after my mother made it clear to me that if I was going to live in her house, I had to attend meetings and do what the Bible said.

So, with no place to go, I packed up my 1991 Mazda Protege and left. Some may say I was kicked out of my home. I like to think I left for greater pastures.

In all of this, I still wasn't fully out and didn't know how to come out. I am sure my mother and family might have had some sort of inkling that I was queer, but up until that point I had never fully said outright that I was queer. Some friends from my old high school knew, and even one of my best friends at the time let me stay with his family until I was able to afford to fully live on campus (thanks, Eric!). But I never did say it or own it the way I fully wanted to.

In my mind, I was going to have a coming-out moment that I had seen on television. I was going to tell my mother, and all would be right in my world – where she would embrace me and there would be some beautiful music that would play in the background.

I was sadly mistaken.

I never had a chance to have that moment because I was forced out of the closet by someone in the Jehovah's Witness organization. I still to this day don't know who it was that spilled my tea and probably will never know who it was or why they did it.

All I know is that when I did finally move on campus for undergrad, I stopped going to the meetings because I began to have a ton of questions about the organization's teachings. I started realizing the ways the organization fed into misogyny.

I began to question why I wasn't given the space to question the teachings and why it seemed that everyone was watching every single move I made.

One day, after someone had left a note on my car, I finally obliged and met with the elders of my congregation. While I knew what they wanted to talk to me about, I never thought that I was also being watched online, too.

Like any millennial in the early 2000s, I used the Internet a lot. But at this time, I was using it a lot more because I finally felt like I had enough freedom to connect with other LGBTQ+ people. As I walked into that meeting and saw all five of the male elders sitting at that table, I knew that they had uncovered my not-so-secret secret.

They passed me a paper that had my profile from XY.com printed on it. They asked me why I was on the site and what it would be like if my family knew. After staring at the paper and looking around the room, I shrugged, owned up to it, and admitted why I was on the site.

While they went back and forth with me about signing some paper that would pretty much take away all my privileges in the Kingdom Hall, I never signed it. I got up, walked out, and never looked back.

■ ■ ■

By the time I was 19, I had finally had enough of watching television and wishing for the world to see me and respect me. I left my religion and my home with the idea that one day I would get to be my authentic self, although I was still getting subtle messages from the media about what it meant to be a Black Fat Femme.

What I call "young social media" – Myspace, Xanga (a space where you could write blogs), and Gay.com – was now where I was getting a lot of my messaging, even though television and film had still built insecurity into me. It was all telling me that I should be happy about being Black while also not being *too* Black because being too Black meant that I was aggressive.

I was being told that I should be proud to be my size but not *too* proud because there is still some shame in being bigger than a size large. That I should be proud to be queer but not *too* proud because I didn't want to be a queen.

It was like I was constantly negotiating the idea that the media was encouraging me to be "my authentic self" while also reminding me that I was some otherworldly thing. Keep in mind that while I'm negotiating all of this, I am watching the ways the media create strange archetypes of Black queer people on television and in film.

The strangest thing about all of early 2000s media was that while it was giving me glimpses of what I thought was the right way to show up as a Black Fat Femme, it was also selling me the idea that being overly confident as a Black Fat Femme somehow made me a problem.

Media never really gave an accurate depiction of what it meant to dive into the lives and experiences of Black Fat Femmes, and often it was always someone else talking about our experiences and rarely anyone who looked or lived like me speaking openly about it.

Anytime I spoke about my feelings of being a Black Fat Femme in college, people made it seem that any representation was good representation and that I should just be happy to have *something*.

I saw how the media fueled the stereotypes I saw of being a Black Fat Femme and how so many of those stereotypes made me fearful of my own performance. The media made me fearful of being or owning the idea of being everything I was taught to hate: being a queen.

One of the hardest things I've had to process in my life is how much hatred effeminate cisgender men get. The thought of any cisgender queer man being a "queen" in my mind has always been fueled by the world's hatred for women. All queer people, specifically Black Fat Femmes, must perform their identity for the eyes of straight people so that they can say they have an understanding of who they are. Think about it – even Ms. J at moments on *America's Next Top Model* fed into this: the quippy and witty candor, the constant need to "throw shade" at every waking moment even if it wasn't called for. This is often only done as a way to make straight people feel safe. What pains me most is feeling like in order for people to like me or love me, I had to play into the stereotypes of what the media had created.

So I became mean. I was catty with an underscore of anger in everything I said and did, knowing that some of it was anger for how I was being treated in the LGBTQ+ community as a Black Fat Femme but mostly it was because of what I saw (and learned) on television. I quickly learned that, to everyone, including myself, Black Fat Femmes weren't people; we were just a character.

At this time I began to believe that being a Black Fat Femme meant one thing: I needed to be unbearably loud to get the attention I was longing for. For years, I had sat in silence because I was always too afraid that someone would know my truth, so now that I was out, I wanted the world to know.

The thing was, I was perceived as "confident" even when on most days I felt I had nothing to be confident about. I became okay with slight digs friends would take at me or my queerness. I was okay with being what I now reflect on as an "accessory" to straight people, specifically straight cisgender (white) women because, again, that is what I saw on *Sex in the City* and *Will & Grace*.

It was about giving the drama in everything, and I wanted everyone to eat it up. I wanted the world to see me!

But little did I know how exhausting and painful pretending to be *that* person would be.

Truth be told: the idea of being queer in the early 2000s was limiting. I was limited to the "gay best friend" and had to live up to every trope that television had fed the world about what it means to be a Black Fat Femme. It came with the expectation of me always needing to be funny. It came with the expectation that I was always going to be ready to do a friend's hair or help her figure out what to wear for some event she might have been embarrassed to take me with her to.

Being a "queen" meant to me that I was everything and nothing all at the same time.

A common thing I began to hear in my day-to-day life was that I was "too much" with people, noting that I always wanted to be the center of attention and took too much of the air and space out of a room. By this time, I had accepted that being "too much" was the thing to be because that was all that I had seen when watching television.

I figured that if people were going to speak poorly about me, I would accept it and be the things that society, specifically television, told me I had to be. Reflecting on that now, I realize that much of what I was doing was just parroting and giving in to the stereotypes of Black Fat Femmes, because outside of what I thought about Luther Vandross and had seen quickly in reference to Andre León Talley, I never had instructions on how I could be like someone that I had seen on television that I actually adored.

While I was searching for someone that I could look to for inspiration in the media, I quickly became aware of who I did not want to be, because I saw the ways people responded to the thought of someone like me "being a queen."

My unlearning of that word being something I hated came in the form of a television show called *Making the Band*. I lived for this show because in the midst of me working multiple jobs and taking insane course loads to try to graduate college early, the show took me back to the place where I was younger, that feeling that television had given me of being my safety net.

The first season was focused on making the boy band O-Town, and I will be frank in saying that I only watched it because I thought Dan, one of the O-Town band members, was hot. I would often get teased by some of my peers in high school for watching it because in the early 2000s, being a reality television junkie wasn't as celebrated or as accepted as it is now. However, I was a diehard pop-culture junkie, and I was looking for anything that would help me escape from the hells of being a young Black queer kid living in the Inland Empire of California.

At the time I became addicted to reality television, *Making the Band* had gone on hiatus for almost four years, and in that time I had almost completely forgotten that the show even existed with all the new reality shows that were out. However, when the show came back, the format was a bit different. After the show found a rap group in the second season, it was now looking for a Black boy and girl group that MTV could market in the same way the network had once marketed O-Town.

I was *sold*.

Seeing the names of the celebs attached to the show made me more excited to watch, mainly because at this time one of the stars, Lauireann Gibson, was a popular choreographer who we all knew was a little off the wall but made absolutely great television. While the first few episodes were built around finding the group producers could work with, by the third episode I was hooked because now I had a true reason to watch as the show had brought a new person into the fold.

Or as my friend noted, "Some *queen* named Jason Williams."

I recall skipping classes some nights to stay home and watch with the girls in the dorm because I didn't want to be out of the loop when everyone began to chat about it the following week. From the first time seeing Jason on the show, it felt like I finally had found someone that mirrored me. While I had seen glimpses of myself in folks like Luther and André over the years, I had never seen someone who I felt so closely related to.

Jason was big like me. He was Black like me. He was overtly effeminate and walked through the doors of the house with such an air of earned confidence that I was still struggling to attain. At this moment, I struggled because it was a bit bittersweet. There were people I would watch the show with who had said they loved me but were responding negatively to Jason on the television.

There were moments in the show where some of the women I had grown to love were also saying really derogatory things about Jason, which sometimes made the show hard to watch. Even in some moments, I didn't want to tell people I liked the show because I was afraid that by saying I watched it, someone would find a reason to say something terrible about Jason, affirming the fears I had in my life that people felt the same way about me.

As the season progressed and I heard more and more terrible things about Jason (both from the contestants and from my friends watching the show), I was committed to trying to convince myself and my peers that Jason's behavior wasn't all that bad. But in my eyes, he was, because I knew all the things people were saying about him both online and off. There was a whole Xanga page dedicated to the hatred for this man someone once shared with me, reminding me that "being a queen" was something I should never want to be.

A specific moment I can recall is him referring to himself as a "den mother" to the girls on the show and my seeing how the women in the house responded to this – and mainly how my friends responded to hearing him say it.

"Girl, he is doing *too much*." I didn't respond because as much as I was happy to see him on the show, I knew what that "too much" meant.

It was me.

It was the loud, boisterous way that I too would show up into a room in college and see people cringe. It was the way he walked into a room and demanded the world to see him, unapologetically. He was "extra" just like me, and while there were moments where it seemed like the world was enjoying it, I knew that finding joy in seeing Jason on the television would be short-lived because people love to tear down Black Fat Femmes.

The notion of being "extra" is something I often would struggle with, because we rarely say that about white queer cisgender men who often take up space. Black Fat Femmes are only "extra" when we show pride in who we are and refuse to let folks demean us. As if the concept of being "extra" and a "queen" are ways to tear down confidence that so many Black Fat Femmes work so hard to build.

For weeks, Jason being a "queen" who was "extra" was all my friends wanted to engage with. "Girl, did you see the way Jason did this/that on the show this week?" Everyone in my dorm was obsessed with *Making the Band*, but not because of the talent the women brought to the show. Not because Jason, a Black Fat Femme, had somehow overcome all the terrible things that people had said and done to him and managed to thrive in being who he was even against all odds. Folks were entertained with the notion of seeing a stereotype play out in front of them. The world wasn't laughing with us. It was laughing at us.

"Girl, Jason is one of my favorite queens!" someone said to me once while watching. I can remember distinctly how bothered I was by this sentiment – and how bothered I was by the ways both I and Jason were talked about. It was like we were great for entertainment value, but no one wanted to understand our plight or our pain.

I can remember actually ending a friendship over this sentiment, where I expressed to someone that calling me (and Jason) a queen only fed into the stereotypes of Black Fat Femmes.

"You're being a queen now!" an ex-friend said to me while we sat at a table for lunch.

I can remember setting down my napkin, drinking from a glass of water, and getting up from the table and leaving. The entire time I drove home I kept thinking to myself that I never wanted to talk to this person again, not because of them calling me a queen but because I knew that in that moment I was just another form of entertainment to them.

■ ■ ■

Even with all the internal bias that I carried around the word *queen*, I was still happy to know that there were people

74

out in the world like Jason Williams who validated my experience. For years I had been teased about how effeminate I was; in this instance, Jason seemed as if the world was celebrating him and all of his fabulousness.

But this is not to say that even with the representation I was starting to see, I wasn't scared to be my authentic self. While – and even now – I had moments where I felt very confident, there were still moments where I wondered if someone was going to say or do something to me that triggered a memory or made me want to regress.

Watching Jason on the show was exactly that. Seeing people almost devour Jason for how queer he was sent coded messages that being a Black Fat Femme was a problem. To so many people I knew, Jason was a joke. But for me – Jason exemplified overcoming. He was able to walk into a room and own every part of himself, something I longed to be able to do.

While so much of me longed for the ability to be as open as I saw Jason being on television, I was terrified to think about the ways being my authentic self would keep me from finding true happiness. I had heard André talk about it. I had seen Luther mention it, but I never had the right words to explain it. What I later learned was that a lot of what I was feeling was homonegativity – the idea that being proud to be queer was in fact wrong.

The hard part about this was that none of it was ever overt. It was also done in a way to make you second guess yourself, often leaving you to be the butt of someone else's joke. I saw it on television often. *Mad TV* was often the most quick to do it – dressing one of their male comedians up to make fun of Jason for being a Black Fat Femme.

What I would later gain in my college journey (outside of my freshman 15) was that being in college and talking to Black queer scholars would give me the verbiage to fully understand the feelings I had, including the struggle to find joy on campus, in the media, and in my life. The word that was given to me by a Black female professor was *intersectionality* – the idea that my identities were fuel for others to oppress me. You know, the intersections of my oppression.

It helped me understand all that was happening including the jokes and the backhanded compliments that I was "not like other gay guys." Mostly, it helped me understand the fear – how I learned it and the moments that I felt like I needed to hide and tuck myself away – and how so much of what I had learned wasn't just something that was picked out of the sky.

The word *intersectionality* led me to learn more about other concepts that would explain why I wanted to stop watching *Making the Band* with my peers. Intersectionality led me to better understand both microaggressions and macroaggressions. It taught me that to most straight cis people, queer folks are often a muse. A clown if you will.

It also helped me better understand fatphobia and femmephobia and how those two ideas intersected in the community.

Most important, being a communications studies major and gender studies minor gave me access to better understand the ways media fueled my internal self-hatred.

I began to see myself as "too womanly." I began to recognize that being Black Fat and Femme was a problem, and I began to try anything and everything I could do to change. Seeing Jason as "big and loud" reminded me of how the world saw me and fueled so much of my internal dialogue.

"You're big, you're loud, and you're obnoxious. No one will ever love you that way."

■ ■ ■

Black. Fat. Femme.

As a Black Fat Femme, it's frustrating to think about how visible you are to the world yet how invisible you are at the same time. If I could say anything about the college experience, much of it was exactly that. I felt that people saw me, but that the world was looking past me. Even in the moments I felt good about myself, subtle hints of racism, anti-Blackness, or femmephobia were lurking in the shadows.

"You're cute for someone your size."

"You're cute for a big boy."

This became something I got used to hearing day in and day out.

It was like I began to pick myself apart before anyone else could. I saw how folks did it to Jason, so it became part of my reality. If I could tear myself down before anyone else did, it would be easier to live with the backhanded compliments.

Considering the subtle shade that people would throw at me and people like him during that time, what silenced a lot of my ideation was knowing that one day I'd get the opportunity to own my identity in the way I saw Jason doing it. Still, that sense of deep-seated fear followed me – especially seeing what so many of my transgender friends were going through and all the backlash LGBTQ+ people were getting because of Prop 8, a California ballot proposition and a state constitutional amendment intended to ban same-sex marriage, which passed in November 2008.

After almost 20 years of deeply hating myself, I just wanted to be happy, and I think that is why I loved Jason so much. Even though the world spoke poorly about him, his existence made me happy. Him taking up space and demanding the respect of others – something I truly didn't know how to do – is what made me such a fan. It was like I was studying him, adding him to the rolodex of Black Fat Femmes who were giving me the roadmap on how to exist.

After weeks watching the show and hearing Jason refer to himself as both a "den mother" and a "queen," I started to believe that maybe being a queen wasn't so bad. It was like I was beginning to have a reckoning with the word and started to understand the power it had. Being a queen meant demanding that people respected you. They didn't have to like you, but they sure as hell better respect you.

Then, on the heels of my last months of college, I began seeing the word "queen" in people's profiles, specifically in gay dating profiles, which I was honestly using to hook up and make friends. Before apps like Grindr and Scruff, there was Gay.com and Adam4Adam.com, a site where you might find booty or your best friend. While I was on these sites looking for love, acceptance, and community (all in the wrong places), I was also getting the subtle message that thinking of myself as the "poor man's Jason Williams" wouldn't save me from a world of hurt. I would read profile after profile and see the same thing over and over. It's almost alarming how casual and common it was to read it.

"NO BLACKS. NO FATS. NO FEMMES. NO QUEENS – PLS."

I knew what these profiles were telling me. That I was everything the world hated and that I needed to pretend to be something else if I was ever going to find someone to love me.

The hard part in seeing this is thinking that for years I experienced hatred from the Black community for being queer, but now I was experiencing racism, fatphobia, *and* femmephobia from a community in which I was hoping to find refuge.

Seeing this over and over began to take a toll on my mental health. I never felt safe. I never felt needed in this world and that is when the ideation I had long ran away from since I was 14 began to kick up again.

"If the world only sees me as a joke, what's the point of living?" was something I would ask myself almost daily. Sometimes hourly.

I remember sharing my feelings with a friend, and he told me to "stop overthinking/being dramatic" about finding a boyfriend when, in reality, I had every reason to feel the way I did.

I was being swallowed up by the idea that nobody would ever want me or ever want to be seen with me because of me "being a queen." I had feelings of never being the attractive person in many of the spaces I moved in, often making me feel like because I refused to play up my masculinity, I was the reason that the world was sending me the subtle messages I was receiving around my identity.

For years, I was fixated on Jason's lived experience and how he became the confident person I saw him projecting on *Making the Band*. Instinctively, while I never met him, I knew he knew my story and could understand everything I had gone through to get to that point in my life.

I had wondered if someone had told Jason, like me, that they "weren't into fat Black guys" Or had told him they weren't into "queens." Or had yelled "eww" at the thought of dancing with him in a club or written "kill yourself" in an Adam4Adam reply message. I was scared most days because I never felt like I would allow myself to live long enough to get to the place that Jason was with his identity.

I wondered if he knew what it was like to be me and how it felt to know that he had that much power to impact folks that he didn't even know.

Chapter 4

The Masc You Live In

"I don't believe in following guidelines. I am gender fluid or gender non-conformist. . . . It means [I] don't adhere to the social norms of society."

—Miss Lawrence

Gender constructs are a funny little thing.

If you ask most people what gender is or where gender began, very rarely can anyone give you a solid answer. Some will say it started with the Bible – but most have no real clue where or why the concept exists.

What's so interesting about all of it is how young it starts. As soon as someone announces they're giving birth, the first question is usually, "Is it a boy or a girl?" At the baby shower everyone gets so excited seeing a specific color attached to the idea of a child. None of this has ever sat well with me, and none of it has ever made any sense to me.

Oddly enough, people uphold the construct and will do anything to make sure you uphold it as well. How many times in your life have you been told "That's for boys" or "That's only for girls"? I can recall times of my childhood being so broken because I wanted to play with Barbie dolls – not because I wanted to be "a girl" but because I always thought (Black) Barbie was awesome. She could be anything. She could *do* anything.

Very rarely did I have anyone telling me that in my own life. I didn't have a figure growing up that reminded me that I could be anything or do anything. That's why I always saw it for Ms. Barbie, because motha was running a whole dynasty while taking care of her sister and babysitting that random Skipper kid.

Barbie was *that girl*. But I digress.

As I got older, I didn't understand that societies wanting me *not* to play with Barbies or do anything feminine was linked to power dynamics, specifically sexism. I would even go further and say that the world hates femininity because they hate women, and that is the reason why so many queer people have a hard time in this life, not because people hate the thought of homosexuality. They hate the thought of a man showing the characteristics of a woman.

I've noted publicly that the hatred effeminate cisgender men get – especially within the queer community – is linked to the disdain the world has for women and how the world looks at womanhood as lesser than manhood. My mother would often try to explain it to me, especially in moments I would share with her the things people were saying to me or the times people wanted to harm me for embracing my effeminate nature.

Then, there's a whole conversation about hypermasculinity, the ways society – specifically media – exaggerates the idea of hegemonic masculinity.

Think 50 Cent for example.

Think of the image of a Black man who doesn't take any crap, is too strong to cry, and will fight at the drop of a dime. All while being emotionally unavailable, angry, and ready to crack at any second. It's sad, because when I think about this trope, I immediately think about all the men in my life who upheld this. Cousins, uncles, and even some of the men my mother married who you could tell were abusive because they never had the agency to be more than a stereotype.

As I regale you with stories about my own growing up, I never understood the need for the world to hypermasculinize men, and specifically young Black men, until I learned that it was all systemic. Thinking about the way the world is set up for Black people, specifically Black men, hypermasculinization of Black cisgender men gives society a reason to go after them when they break free from the trap of suppressing their anger – or run from the stereotype like I did.

So much of this understanding came from the conversations I had with my mother, who knew exactly what the world was trying to do. She would often remind me of what white supremacy was doing in the world and how it was having an impact on her.

I'd be remiss if I didn't mention that so much of my (now) better understanding of the ways the world treated Black men (and Black people) came from watching the ways the world treated my mother. While I knew early in my life that so much of my lived experience would be different because of cisgender male privilege, people still to this day say I act like my mother.

And that I do, because my mother is and will always be that girl.

My mother didn't take anything from anyone. Not from men. Not from white people, and definitely not from people who thought they could disrespect her because they held a position of power. I watched her, and because I always looked up to her, I wanted to be just like her. Still to this day, my mother is me and I am she. But, in me being "just like her," I quickly learned how much the world didn't like women like her. The world didn't like Black women like her, and they damn sure didn't like Black boys who acted like her.

This taught me early on in my life why and how the world hates women (specifically Black cis women and Black trans women). It helped me understand how and why the world responded to me, not just because I was effeminate but because I spoke out against heteronormativity and sexism. I felt it then, and I always feel it now.

To the world, the thought of a young Black boy living in peril by not tucking his feelings away was unfathomable. This is why queer Black boys have such a hard time in life. This is why I had a hard time growing up. The world knew I knew I had been taught the tricks of the game and wasn't going to fall victim to toxic masculinity.

Though I can't speak for every queer cisgender Black man in my story, I have spoken with several who noted that doing anything remotely feminine was almost a death sentence for them. On so many occasions in my life I "butched" myself up just so I could keep myself from being beat up or harassed by a group of not-so-straight men (if you know, you know).

I would look for anything and everything that made me seem a little more manly. This meant looking for other queer people in my life who also played up their masculinity too. I was desperate to appear more masculine because I was so tired of being treated poorly by the world for appearing too "girly."

Then come the moments – even now – where I can feel myself hiding my nails or struggling with what bathroom I have to use, all because I don't want to deal with people trying to decode my presentation. It gets exhausting. It's been exhausting.

Some folks are so committed to the concept of gender, and so much of our trauma as people, specifically queer Black people, is wrapped up in the idea of gender because folks can't see anything past "male" or "female." They have an idea that I, as a queer nonbinary person, can't exist beyond the small glass box that you have put yourself and others in. Something as reductive as contact lenses can cause a man trying to uphold masculinity to have a meltdown.

You read that right. Contact lenses.

I can recall when I was about 11, I had to start wearing glasses daily because my vision was slowly deteriorating and I was having a hard time focusing in class. I knew my mother wore contact lenses, so instead of wanting to wear glasses, I asked if I could try wearing contacts.

The thought of being able to see without glasses was always so cool to me, especially knowing that being called "four eyes" was something I didn't want to add to the long list of names people were already calling me.

More than anything, I really wanted contact lenses specifically because I had seen how one of my peers was treated after he got glasses. Kids would hide them or do things to try to break them. After what felt like weeks of me making my case, my mother got on board with me getting contact lenses because I was diligent about how I took care of my reading glasses – or anything that I considered really important in my life because we truly didn't have much of anything nice.

The caveat of me wanting contact lenses? I only wanted them if I could have them in color. I wanted the gray Air Optix with three-in-one color technology. I wasn't playing any games.

You would have thought I was asking my mother to put me in drag. My father, who at the time was *very* absent from my life, lost his cool. "Young boys don't need to be in colored contacts! The's gay!!" And it wasn't just him saying it. It was my uncles and cousins too.

The Masc You Live In

All I could hear every time I thought about putting them on was, "That's for girls!"

In the late '90s, colored contacts were all the rage, and I thought it was so cool seeing my mother being able to change her whole look just by changing the color of her eyes. However, in my father's mind, my mother letting me wear colored contacts was just feeding into the idea that somehow a piece of prescription plastic in my eyes was going to make me "look and act like a girl."

There was so much contention around the idea that I, a young Black boy, wanted to do something he saw his mother doing. In reality, it was simply gender politics playing out – specifically the idea that my father, at the time, thought that if he puffed out his chest enough, somehow I would "man up" or at least fear doing anything that he (or the world) considered womanly.

This made life heavy. It made every moment, interaction, second of my life feel like I needed to exemplify the perfect representation of what it meant to be a man, even though I was just a kid. I had spent most of my life hearing people tell both me and my mother that I needed to "man up," but I never really understood what that meant. Still to this day I have yet to understand it.

But this wouldn't be the first time I felt this energy, this cold hand placed on my back telling me that I needed to act or be more manly. For years, I got the same message from friends, from my family, and even from school teachers.

That's right.

I had a teacher once call me a girl in front of the classroom in the seventh grade. His exact words?

"I really wish you would stop acting like a girl. You always act like a faggot."

I remember other students laughing at me. I remember my cousin being in the class and her laughing with the boy who bullied me, to the point where I almost took my own life. I can also remember how irate it made my mother, sending her down to my school to almost fight the teacher who said it. While I was a bit embarrassed by the way my mother cursed him out (I've never heard or seen her go off like that until that day), it was a stark reminder of how the world would treat me for the rest of my life.

In all, these stories shaped a big part of how I felt about myself growing up, but mainly how I felt about my own effeminate nature. Gender performance is something that has always given me the most trouble, and even to this day I struggle with it because I always wonder if (or when) someone is going to challenge it and if I will have the capacity to act in a rational manner.

Dealing with the feeling that you always have to perform masculinity is something that has always exhausted me and, frankly, is part of the reason why I now lean into being nonbinary. It offers me a place to just exist without the gross feeling of putting on a persona that I and others know is fake.

But it's not just the idea of "performance" that makes it tough. It's the moments where I have to move and exist in a world that never really knows what to do with someone like me. It's also the moments that I can clearly see the world demanding I conform, even when I feel like I have made it clear that I have no interest.

My nails are intentional. The way I dress and even how I sometimes sink into my effeminate nature is resistance because I know that doing so throws a wrench into the system. I will admit that it is hard, and sometimes I struggle with being confident in my own chosen way to perform in this world.

It's having to think about how I am going to get someone to understand my pronouns. It's the times I am on the phone and have to argue with a representative to get them to let me make changes to my account because I "don't sound like Mr. Higgins." It's the moments I can tell someone is looking at me and trying to figure out "what I am" and if I am using the right restroom.

It's the stares I get when I am sitting in the nail shop and people wonder why "a man" would want to get his nails done because "that is for girls." It's being followed and stopped when I am in the big girl section of Target as I am looking for something I can feel good in and being asked, "Can I help you find something for your wife?" knowing what the worker is inferring.

I often think about how cisgender men rarely have the opportunity to explore and define themselves on their own terms and how lonely that can be. From childhood, masculinity is enforced through phrases like "boys will be boys," setting harmful precedents before individuals even grasp the concept of gender.

I even think about the moments of how this shapes the interactions I have had in the queer community in my earlier years, how I often tucked parts of my femininity away in hopes that someone would read me as "masculine" and find me attractive.

I've struggled with my own rage and emotional unavailability for years, all because I truly didn't know how to perform or simply didn't want to.

For years, I've delved into the complexities of "manhood," researching and writing extensively, only to conclude that the term itself is not just problematic but inherently dangerous. The very idea that we exist in a world where children, still trying to figure out who they are, are instructed to "act like a man" speaks volumes about society's perception of femininity.

I've long voiced my belief that society hates women, which significantly complicates the existence of cis and trans women alike. Matters become even more convoluted when race enters the chat and reminds Black men, specifically young Black men, that they have to adhere to not only the confines of the culture but to the expectations of society as well.

I quickly learned that gender constructs were everywhere and the full intention was for people to use them to make my life a living hell.

The hardest part about being young, Black, and what I know now as gender-fluid is all the heat you get from folks who claim to care about you. Once as a teen I was told by someone in the church that if I acted "less like a girl, people would treat [me] better." Imagine hearing that and not knowing what to do with it.

I mean, I was use to being teased, but at this point in my life I didn't understand why me being a little "softer" than other boys would cause people to treat me the way they did. Then I realized that it was because the world didn't want me to be. It wanted me to be cold, mean, and angry. It wanted me to take everything that had happened to me in life and funnel it into my actions. The interesting thing about this time in my life was that even with all the pushback I got for being "soft," I never let it take away the joy I had in my spirit. I knew that the world was going to always be mean to me for how I presented, so I constantly told myself, "Don't lose that spark that the world is working so hard to put out."

The spark that I saw in other gender-queer people, like Miss Lawrence, a singer, activist, and actress who had started out doing hair and eventually took over television, reminded me that soon the world would see the beauty in my gender nonconformity. That's not to say I didn't continue to struggle to understand what made me different in a life that I felt constantly reminded me that I was in fact different.

By the time I graduated college, I had no idea who I was or who I wanted to be because I simply didn't know *how* to just *be*. Up to that point, my entire life was filled with subtle (and not so subtle) messages that something was wrong with me because I didn't present in the traditional way boys did.

I was struggling to make sense of why the world was so cold to me when I simply wanted to just be my authentic self. However, up to this point, I realized that I had been wearing multiple masks in order to make others comfortable with who I was, only to realize I did it because I truly didn't *know* who I was or who I wanted to be.

I thought a lot of it was tied to the fact that I lacked true masculine energy in my life. But the reality was that I was afraid of it. I never felt safe around masculinity. Even now when I am around men who I assume are cisgender and straight identifying, I worry either that my presentation will be questioned or that I may have to "buck up." Yes, I may have to sharpen my tongue or clench my fist because there might be someone ready to hurt or harm me.

Even as I wrote my dissertation and included concepts of what I called "Mask-u-linity" – the concept of cisgender queer Black men masking their true identity – I was still trying to figure out why I was so afraid to be read as gender-queer.

Even as I write this, there are times I freeze in my queerness or put the gender mask back on. Sometimes I lower my voice so people won't read me as a woman on the phone or at a drive-through. Other times I simply order clothes online so I don't have to deal with the stares as I shop in the women's section.

So much of gender constructs is the worry or fear that someone is going to judge you for not performing as expected.

In fact, a lot of my life has been one big performance, specifically when it comes to gender and my own gender identity. Until my early 20s, I had actually become comfortable with the ways in which my family dictated my presentation, with how religion was molding me to be the "ideal man," and with not being "man enough" for other men in the LGBTQ+ community.

Considering that I was a media junkie, I was also garnering messages from television and film about the way I should present and the idea that if I was clocked as being overly effeminate in an unsafe environment, I might experience harm.

I had seen how the media treated queer people. I had seen the ways in which the media had written trans characters, and my biggest fear was being treated in the ways I saw my genderqueer and trans counterparts being treated. So I did what so many effeminate queer people do. I "butched" myself up.

But doing this only made life more complicated. I was always wondering if someone would see the parts of me that were more feminine and scream "Gotcha!" I knew I was lying to myself about who I was and who I really wanted to be. Deep in my heart, I knew there was a joy that lived in me in being able to walk the line of both masculinity and femininity in a way that most people would never be able to do.

My personal journey has led me to question the hostility toward cis men who exhibit effeminate traits and why I – like so many of my Black Fat Femme counterparts – must always present in a way that makes others comfortable while leaving so many of us feeling trapped in an idea of who the world wants us to be versus who we truly *want* to be.

My conclusion is that gender constructs were created in order for systems of oppression to continue to work.

Think about it: if the world can tell me, a Black cis man, how to dress, talk, and perform, then it is easy to control every other part of my life too. However, by me presenting as nonbinary and telling the world to go F itself, I am in turn pushing back against years of white supremacy and more, controlling my own lived narrative in a way that most queer people never get to do.

Being nonbinary for me has meant freedom. Freedom that has never been afforded to Black people – Black women and Black men alike.

While societal constructs heavily influence gender performance, the world has afforded men no room to embrace the parts of femininity that can often be so freeing, because folks know what it means for me to embrace said freedom.

The world hates me because being a Black Fat Femme has afforded me freedom.

For years, while I thought it was a curse that people read me as effeminate, I quickly learned that said curse was in fact my superpower all along.

■ ■ ■

By 2009 I had graduated college and was living on my own, fully ready to come into my own. I was still battling with issues around my identity, but mentally I was in a place where I knew that if I didn't come to terms with the intersections of my identity, the constant hatred and talking down to myself was going to kill me.

I was going to kill me.

So I told myself, "Suck it up, Buttercup, and be who you are. The world is going to judge you no matter what you do." I knew that the only way I could save my own life would be to embrace the parts of me that were easiest to love – the thing that made me, me.

That thing I know now as my nonbinaryness.

While some might believe from reading past chapters that accepting my femininity might have been the hardest thing for me to come to terms with, it actually wasn't as much of an uphill battle than you might think. I was already into makeup. I had already started learning how to walk in heels and was even okay with adding some (light) color to my nails.

I had already begun to accept that the world was always going to see me as "girly," so I figured, why not give in to it? However, the hardest part about it was living in what I call a bubble. I didn't see anyone else who looked or lived the way I wanted to.

Then I was introduced to Miss Lawrence and Derek J. Yes, the fashion and makeup icons on TV.

While the world was latching on to all things Atlanta at that time and *Real Housewives of Atlanta* was on the tip of everyone's tongue, I actually didn't know who either of them were at the time or the impact that they were having on the world.

The best thing about seeing Miss Lawrence on *Real Housewives* was how sure of herself she was. It didn't feel fake. It never looked forced. I never saw someone on television look so comfortable in their skin, and while Miss Lawrence might not have been a Black Fat Femme, she was still Black and femme and giving legendary vibes.

My introduction to Derek J began with the film *Good Hair*. For those who are unfamiliar, the film is set in Atlanta, Georgia, and follows several hair stylists who are competing at Bronner Bros hair show. What was so important at that moment in time was to see Derek J – who *is* a Black Fat Femme – in kinship with other Black femmes and thriving in their day-to-day life.

Beyond the celebrity that both of these individuals brought to my life, it reminded me that there were other Black Fat Femmes out there who truly wanted to see me win. They wanted to uplift me and remind me that I didn't have to silence myself to be digestible, which was so important for me at this time in my life.

For years, I really sat with how lonely I felt. I felt like there would never be any other person in the world who would not only get my passion for entertainment but my want to be myself. Seeing the kinship that Miss Lawrence and Derek J had at that time not only comforted me but reminded me how important community would be in my life and, more, how important it is to own my personal power.

While I would get glimpses across my Myspace and Facebook timelines occasionally and see folks work with Miss Lawrence and Derek J, seeing both of them on *Real Housewives* (and in media in general) told me that I didn't have to sink – meaning, tuck myself away from the world. It also afforded me the ability to stand a little bit taller and to walk with my head a bit higher.

Basically, seeing both of them reminded me to stand taller.

Up to this point, I had never seen (or heard) Black queer people so rightfully demand that people respect them. Watching them catch people's snide remarks about their size or their queerness and checking them in real time was huge for me.

For years, I had let people make a joke out of my queerness. I had let folks say and do things to me that I know now are micro- and macroaggressive – without speaking up to defend myself. For almost two years of my life, I had let a "friend" refer to me as "G-Jon," only to learn that "G" stood for "gay."

I never stood up for myself because I never knew how. Watching Miss Lawrence and Derek J on television afforded me the opportunity to see two Black femmes instruct others on how to treat them. They demanded people respect their names as well as the work they had put into affirming themselves both personally and professionally.

Watching them at this time in my life was more than entertainment. It was a lesson on owning my personal power in a way that life had never afforded me the ability to. Until that time, I never realized how much I really needed them to lay that out for me and how seeing them at that point in time in my life was literally the lifesaver that I needed.

Seeing both of them in the film *Good Hair* and dominating the television both in the *Real Housewives* and in their *Fashion Queens* television show let me know it was time to take back the idea that the world got to delegate not just how I showed up but how I let folks treat me. Seeing them was a stark reminder that I had the power to tell others what they could and couldn't do to me and what boundaries people could and couldn't cross.

Up to this point in my life, I had never seen two Black queer people being unapologetically Black Fat Femme and demanding others to make space for them. I had never seen Black Fat Femmes demanding the world to receive them and respect this.

I never even thought it was possible. I never felt as if I had the right. It was as if I had finally seen two people who I para-socially knew crack the code. They told me that it was possible to be seen and even reverenced.

Seeing them told me that I had the right to not just like who I am but to *love* who I am after years of secretly believing that since the world hated me, I had to do the same. It's hard to even put into words what that even felt like because it was a feeling I never thought I'd ever have in my lifetime.

Even when the world tried to make Miss Lawrence and Derek J out to be a joke, they would come right back around and flip the joke on its head. A joke isn't a joke if the person you are laughing at is in on it – and watching them I quickly learned that.

I didn't comprehend the harm in the jokes because I never really had the time or the emotional capacity to do so. This is something so common for all marginalized people; we sometimes let harm slide because we know that we don't have the emotional capacity to acknowledge and handle our harm while teaching others about why something they do or say is harmful. We tuck each of these "ouches" away, only for something else to come along to push another one down to make room for it.

It's a constant cycle that never ends.

I never recognized how being an accessory to folks felt good because I was so desperate to be accepted. I knew that people – specifically women – saw me as "the gay friend" because of the media, but seeing Miss Lawrence and Derek J on my television screen reminded me that being a Black Fat Femme meant so much more.

■ ■ ■

When I mention both Miss Lawrence and Derek J's names to people (specifically white people), folks just write them off as people who work in the industry. I have made the same mistake, because the world (and media) has a way of playing down the impact that certain Black Fat Femmes have on this world.

What makes Miss Lawrence and Derek J the legends that they are isn't just their impact on both fashion and the television industry. It's that they were living and thriving in a time when the world was too afraid to acknowledge the importance that nonbinary people make in the media.

Watching them and learning from both of them taught me that in our world, stereotypes are created to control people. Stereotypes make people think less about their identities so that they conform in order for someone else to maintain power.

But seeing Miss Lawrence and Derek J not only be pretty but be confident in their pretty rocked my world because it told me that I had the power to be in control. It told me that even if I am "too much," I had the right to be. It taught me that if being my authentic self made others uncomfortable, that was not my problem.

When Miss Lawrence and Derek J were making a name for themselves, they opened doors for folks like activist and media mogul B. Scott of LoveBScott.com fame, who too reminded me that there was nothing wrong with being "pretty."

For years, I hated being called that because I knew what people meant. "He's gay."

I always saw it as a slight dig. It was a way for folks to say the quiet thing that they didn't agree with out loud: that I was "too much" or that I was feeding into the stereotype that all gay men wanted to be women.

It opened my eyes to the notion that some cisgender men choose to show up as pretty, not because they are putting on a show but because gender performance as a whole is in fact a messed-up construct. Seeing Miss Lawrence and Derek J told me that after years of beating myself up for my gender presentation, I could let that construct go. I had the right to be free. Seeing them on screen, being unapologetically themselves, sends a powerful message: I have a place in this world. Not just to exist but to flourish.

The concept of thriving felt alien to me for the longest time because my life seemed like a constant struggle. Finding joy and embracing my identity seemed like distant dreams. Their presence in the media serves as a beacon of hope, a reminder that embracing every facet of who I am is not just acceptable but essential. It's a revelation that the world might actually respond positively to me owning what I now know as my nonbinary identity.

Their journeys give me courage, a sense of belonging, and the belief that maybe, just maybe, I can carve out my own space in this world that so often told me that I didn't have the right to live. It was right there on the screen in front of me.

Miss Lawrence and Derek J, two Black Fat Femmes, were doing exactly that. Living.

Their visibility challenges societal norms and celebrates diversity, showing that there's no one-size-fits-all approach to identity or expression. They redefine beauty standards and break barriers, inspiring countless individuals, myself included, to embrace our authentic selves without fear or apology. In a world that often tries to box us into rigid categories, their boldness and resilience are a breath of fresh air, reminding us

Derek J (left) and me at G.L.A.A.D.'s Inaugural Black Creatives of Color Conference in Beverly Hills, California

that our differences are not flaws to be hidden but strengths to be celebrated.

As I continue on my own journey of self-discovery and acceptance, I hold their legacy with me, grateful for the courage they've instilled in me and hopeful for a future where everyone can live their truth openly, loudly, and proudly.

Me and Miss Lawrence (right) at the Inaugural ForbesBLK in Atlanta, Georgia

Five Gs, Please!

"Good God, get a grip, girl!"

—Latrice Royale

My whole life I've struggled with my weight. The most interesting part about my struggle is how it felt like no one ever talked about it because I was a "man" and "men don't talk about their weight."

Oh, but they do.

I can recall moments in grade school, hearing boys go back and forth about the insane things they were doing to "make weight" for sports. Some of them would stop eating. Some of them would do things that I now know as binge eating.

Want something to bulk up? Talk to the coach of the football team.

Want to slim down? Go join track and run several miles a day. Many of them had eating disorders, but because so many of them were "in shape," people overlooked it and pretended that it never existed. At one point I even joined cross country, not because I enjoyed running, but because I got so tired of both kids in school and my family making fun of how much weight I had put on.

I wasn't supposed to do extracurricular activities because of my religion, but I was practically forced into sports because not only did all the men in my family play football, but I was fat and apparently I wasn't doing enough to get the weight off.

The easiest way to lose the weight was to join the track team (or so I thought), and even then I wasn't losing the weight fast enough. It was like my mind could never rest. I was always thinking about either my sexuality or my size. Thus, the only way to get my mind to rest was to eat.

While society and media works overtime to make us think that men aren't thinking about their size, trust me when I say it's something that men, specifically cis men, do think about; and it's even more prominent when you are queer.

My weight became an even bigger deal to me by the time I got to college, to the point where I was spending two to three hours a day working out. Even worse, I was working out almost seven days a week – eight if you count the days that I worked out twice.

I then began limiting my calories to a little over 1,500 calories per day and working out to burn more than 2,000 calories so I was constantly in a caloric deficit. Health didn't matter to me. I wanted to be thin, and I was willing to do anything to achieve it.

This began to cause my relationship with food to spiral. There would be nights that I would practically starve myself and then go to Jack in the Box and order $50 worth of burgers, tacos, and fries all to sit there and eat it by myself. Then I would wake up the next morning and go work out, feeling guilty about how much I ate the night before.

Some nights I would go clubbing with friends and pretty much starve myself the entire day with the idea that I wanted to look as thin as possible while I was out. Then, I would get home at 3 a.m. and order a ton of food from Del Taco because I was practically starving.

Let's also not forget the nights that I would stay up late studying with peers and would order a $5 pizza and eat the whole thing. Or the time that I went vegetarian because someone told me that it helped them lose a bunch of weight.

Yes, since I was a teenager my relationship with my body and food has always been unhealthy, and even now at my big age I am still wrestling with what I now know as both body dysmorphia and food addiction. Even writing this, you could say that I have an eating disorder, and I wouldn't even fight you on it.

While I could lie and say "I have no idea where my obsession with food and my weight came from," I can pinpoint the very moments I started to realize that it was going to be a problem. It was the first time I saw SlimFast in the kitchen cabinet. It was also the first time I saw an Overeaters Anonymous book on an aunt's kitchen table and learning that she was addicted to eating reduced-fat frozen yogurt. It was also going to different family members' houses and there being a designated time for the kitchen to be "closed," meaning "Keep your big a$$ out of my refrigerator."

Anytime I told anyone in my family that I was hungry, it was always "Eat some fruit" or "Drink some water." That was a subtle way of folks saying that I was too big without actually having to say it. Ironically, my family would forever go to buffets, specifically HomeTown Buffet, and I would practically be forced to eat anything and everything I put on my plate.

But then folks would make fun of me for how much I ate. This would in turn only make me want to eat more, so whenever I got my hands on something I loved (e.g. butter pecan ice cream), I would eat the entire carton.

Never mind the time I got in trouble for doing exactly that: eating an entire carton of butter pecan ice cream in one day.

But it wasn't just me who had issues with overeating. Growing up, I recognized that many people in my family were always on some type of diet. Low carb this and sugar free that. I even had a family member take me to the gym when I was 12 forcing me to run and lift weights. It was like the world was looking for any and every way to shrink me, and even now, I still feel the pressure.

Even though my family never talked about it openly or directly, everyone in my life touted the same message: don't be too Black or too queer, but most importantly, *don't be fat*.

For years, I watched my aunts, my cousins, and my mother go toe to toe with their weight. I even remember hearing my family talk openly about one of my aunts going under the knife to lose weight and me considering doing the same thing once I was old enough to get a doctor to do it. Though much of these conversations were never directly with me, the rhetoric of "don't get fat" always danced around me.

Even when I would go to spend the night at a cousin's house, I can remember my aunts and cousins policing how much I was eating. "Jon, why are you always in the kitchen?" someone might say. Or, someone would make a comment about food being gone and someone else would point their finger at me as the culprit. But no one ever really stopped to ask me when I was younger *why* I ate a lot or why I was always so hungry.

When I talk about my battle with food and food addiction, I always start the conversation with talking about food instability first. Yes, we like to shame fat people for being fat, but I'm sure that if you talk to a fat person, I am almost certain that they would tell you that their want or need to eat stems from the fear of lack of food.

Food was gold in our house because, honestly, it was (one) of the ways I knew my mother loved me. It was also the way we celebrated.

Got a good grade on a test? Eat.

Landed your first job? Eat.

You didn't get a girl pregnant? Eat.

When momma cooked, *she cooked the house down boots.* It wasn't just spaghetti. It was also a chef salad, homemade garlic bread, and a dessert to follow. She often made everything from scratch. Dinner was usually the biggest meal of our day, but I can also remember going on school field trips and my mother packing me what I felt like was a cannon of a lunch box: two sandwiches, two bags of chips, a big bottle of Gatorade, and two honey buns. Her favorite words?

"I don't want my baby to be hungry!" And we never were, at least not from what I can remember. Even at times my mom was unsure about how she was going to keep food in the house, we ate. It may not have been what we wanted, but I can honestly say that we never went hungry.

While many of my family memories are rooted around food, I knew I was overweight before I even knew or understood what it meant for me to be queer. My family celebrated with food because that was just a way of life. Eating made us all feel good, and often it signaled that things in life were semi-okay.

Usually, seeing a full fridge either meant we had the money for food or meant it was a month that we knew that mom wasn't having trouble with her food stamps. The struggle was always keeping said refrigerator full, which was what often led me to overeat. I was always worried that I was going to go hungry, even though I knew that my mother was doing every-thing in her power to keep my brother and I fed.

The fear that always lived in me was knowing that food was something that I might have to fight over in the long run, espe-cially because there were moments in my life where I knew we had it but we just needed to make it stretch. All in all, my mother was amazing at keeping me and my brother with food in our stomachs, but that is where some of the problem began.

The most interesting thing is that it felt like everyone in my family was always battling weight issues, and somehow, this was normalized. No one ever stopped to acknowledge the relationship we had with our bodies and with food/food insecurity.

No one wanted to admit it, but we all were eating to sup-press the oppression we faced. We were eating to get away from the stress of being Black, poor, and what I know now as systematically marginalized.

Though, there was so much joy when we got together and cooked. My mother made the best potato salad. My uncles fried the best chicken and could make the best bar-b-que that you've ever had. My late uncle Larry would make the best (and deadliest) peach cobbler that had so much sugar and butter in it, it would put Paula Deen to shame.

My family may have been awful at times to deal with, but when it came to food, they always got it right.

Rarely was anyone in my family a bad cook (except for one of my aunts, bless her heart). Even if someone was a bad cook, they knew to bring something to the function that was tasty because they didn't want to get roasted for being a bad cook.

The irony was that my family would cook a lot of food and shame you for how much food you had on your plate at the same time. Make it make sense.

I can't recall anyone in my family ever being successfully thin. If they were, everyone was talking behind their back about how they got thin or what they were doing to stay that way.

My momma's other favorite thing to say? "You know they're thin because they are on that stuff." Stuff meaning drugs or, "You know she got that surgery."

Surgery was the lap band – something I constantly thought about getting – even though I was only 15. I would go back to having the idea of wanting to do anything to be slim prior to the pandemic – until my surgery was postponed due to COVID and canceled after I decided that I wasn't mentally prepared for it.

Some days I regret that decision. Some days I am proud of myself for not giving into the pressure I was putting on myself to be thin. Although I am happy with my decision, the thought of being slim is something that has always lived in the back of my mind, and I often worry that it might not ever fully go away.

■ ■ ■

If I said that growing up in the 2000s didn't have an impact on my mental health and my issues around my body image, I would totally be lying. It was like everywhere you turned, someone was talking about how skinny someone in the media was, or how fat someone.

I often think about the messaging I got, specifically around the time that Billy Blanks and Tae Bo became a thing. It was every-where, and I can remember recording it on my VCR so that I could study what Billy Blanks was doing so I could do it in my room.

The truth was, I wanted to be skinny and desirable. I thought in my teenage years that if I could lose weight, not only would my life get better but that people – specifically my peers and family – would stop teasing me.

Five Gs, Please!

The biggest taunting around my weight started with my uncle, who constantly reminded me how big I was getting. Considering I *was* almost 300 lbs by the time I was 16, my family would comment that it was because I was "lazy" and not doing enough of what the "other boys were doing." This being code for "you're not manly enough."

This is when I was forced (again) to play football, not *just* because I needed to be more manly, but because it would help me lose weight. As much as I hated the thought of going to practice (which I never did and ended up getting in trouble for wasting my uncle's money), I still felt so much pressure to lose weight, which caused me to be more sad/depressed, which then would lead me to eat even more. It was such a vicious cycle.

But the truth was that so much of my desire to overeat was also driven by my fear of being found out to be queer and being teased for not acting *or* looking like other boys my age. If I wasn't being teased for how "girly" I was, I was being teased for how big I was. Thus, I would get back on my Ferris wheel of emotional eating, looking for anything and everything I could find to make me feel better – even if it lasted the duration of what it would take for me to wolf down two bags of chili cheese Fritos with extra chili and extra cheese.

Now, with years (and a lot of money) spent in therapy, I recognize *why* I have a really unhealthy relationship with both my body and with food, and it is still something that I am working through. I still have to catch myself when I get happy that someone says I look thinner. I have to also catch myself on days I am sad and I want to beast an entire box of Krispy Kreme donuts. Sometimes I have to remind myself why I am eating or working out more than normal.

While I have learned to control that little voice in my head that constantly calls me fat, I have also come to understand where it stems from. It's a little word that my therapist calls addiction.

As I have gotten older, I have come to realize that society centers so much of the conversation around addiction as solely being on drugs and alcohol, but food is truly just as terrible. In America, so much of the food you eat is pumped full of preservatives that are truly unhealthy for you, but at the same time, food that is "healthy" for you is damn near impossible to afford or often hard to get to.

Let's also add that there is an extra layer of time: the healthier the food is often means minimally processed, which means it takes more time to prep and cook than something you can just throw in the microwave for a few minutes. So if you are working 40+ hours a week (or 50+ in my case) and commuting to work, in school, or have children, then God bless you if you have time to cook for yourself and/or your family when you get home.

But I digress.

It's easy for me to talk about addiction because it wasn't something that my mother or her father hid from me, which I am truly grateful for. My mother would often tell me in my younger years, specifically when I was a teenager, that it is easy to become addicted to pretty much anything if you don't watch it. For some in my family, it was drugs.

For my mother and grandfather, it was alcohol.

For me, it was (and still is) food. While some might say that I got off easy, it really is something that I wish people would talk about more because it really *is* a much bigger problem than what we acknowledge.

Now, before I go on, I do want to make it clear that I don't believe that *all* fat people are addicted to food or that fat people have some kind of issue with food or their size. What I am saying is that my journey with food hasn't been easy, and it has a lot to do with the unhealthy relationship I have with my body and the way I view myself.

Like my grandfather and a few others in my family, I am and have always suffered from addiction, and up until 2023, it was hard for me to admit that.

I never thought anyone could have a food addiction. However, after returning to therapy after the guilt I had from gaining back all the weight I had lost to get approved for bariatric surgery, my therapist helped me say it: I am a food addict. I am addicted to the feeling that food gives me.

She helped me understand that addiction can take many forms, and while my family opted to use drugs and alcohol to ease their woes, I traded my interest in drugs and alcohol for food. She helped me understand that pastries are my drug of choice. For years, I never fully understood why until my therapist helped me understand it better.

Beyond the high food gives me, it also made me feel safe. Yes, food instability is also a *big* part of why I relish food the way I do, but I liken it to the reasons why people go out and get drunk. Food, specifically desserts, gives me that same type of feeling. The sweet taste of sugar just does something for me. It's that feeling that you get from a good kiss or a good lay – that's what food, specifically a good cake or donut does for me.

There is nothing like it. Even writing about it now and thinking about it fills me with joy because I love it so much. Also, desserts are linked to some of the grander memories I have growing up.

It's a running joke on the Internet that all Black people need "a little something sweet" after their meals, which was a way I knew things were good growing up. My mother was (and still is) a great cook. She was even better when it came to making and baking desserts.

Coming home after a long day and hearing her say "Don't make too much noise. I don't want my cake to fall" was music to my ears. Not only did it tell me to expect something good after dinner, but it told me that we actually *had* food.

Eating desserts with my mother and my brother in our home after a good meal was something holy. It was like going to church (or Kingdom Hall) for me. More than anything, it became a moment where I could let my shoulders down and un-tense my back. I knew food wouldn't tease me or make me feel a certain way because I wasn't feeding into toxic masculinity. I knew food wouldn't out me or make me feel like I wasn't "man enough" for masking my emotions.

In so many ways, food was the only thing that never made me feel unlovable. Even on my worst day, food just somehow made everything better. It allowed me to feel good, even if the high from it lasted no longer than a few bites. Now I have come to accept that I will always have a messed-up relationship with food.

I eat when I am sad, then I get sad about how much I eat, so I eat again. Around and around I go.

The thought – or might I say obsession – with my size only became more inherent when I came out. In college, I spent way more time online and in the clubs than in the classroom because, truthfully, I just wanted to be in community with other people who I believed understood me and wouldn't judge me for being queer.

Until they did.

Baby, being Black Fat Femme in queer spaces was almost more hurtful than living in the closet. I was getting subtle messages – both online and off – that not just my race but my size was an issue.

Quick pivot: The worst part of my coming out was coming out during what I call the "Abercrombie era." Yes, this was the era in history where everyone wanted to be "white hot," and even if you were Black, you were doing anything and everything you could to lessen the chances of being called a "nigger" by another white queen.

So, I did what most Southern California queer Black kids were doing, braving (and bracing for) the racism that I would experience both in West Hollywood, California, and Hillcrest in San Diego, California.

Much of my undergrad years I spent going to Tigerheat and Rage in West Hollywood hoping that by some lucky chance I would find community and hoping that this would lead me to be like the singer Usher and find love in the club. But boy was I wrong. I only found heartache because most, if not every, interaction I had with someone (typically white) in the club led to me feeling even worse about my identity, specifically my size.

I was looking for community, love, and acceptance anywhere I could find it and would always go home ready to cry because by the end of the night, I felt so damn ugly.

Talk to any Black Fat Femme and they will tell you. It's not something someone says or does to you inadvertently. It's just a feeling you get when you are in these spaces. You know from jump that you are not wanted or welcome. Even if you are confident in who you are, you still have to damn near fight to stay confident in these spaces. It's like the entire world saw me, but didn't see at all. It's hard to explain, but if you know, you know.

Considering that at this time twinks were always the focal points at both these clubs, I would often go and just dance in a corner by myself. In my mind, no one ever wanted to dance with me or honestly be seen dancing near me. Now it makes me sad to think I thought so little of myself.

I'll never forget the night I was feeling my oats and thought I could get on one of the boxes to dance. A security guard pulled me down because he was afraid I was going to break it. I was so embarrassed that I went home early.

But it wasn't just in clubs. It was online too. Let me tell you: while apps like Grindr and Scruff might seem bad now, they were *worse* back in the early 2010s. I'm talking about randomly getting messages that you were ugly just sitting in your inbox because you existed on the apps.

Let's also remember that you used to be able to filter the demographic of men you were interested in based on race and weight and there were practically no options available for non-binary or trans people.

Wild times indeed.

It was like almost every single profile had "No Fats" in it. Yeah, the "No Blacks" and "No Femmes" thing bothered me, but for some reason "No Fats" always struck a much deeper trigger. I think partly because I knew Blackness and queerness were out of my control. However, my weight – that was a different story.

More than anything, what made that time hard was that I didn't have the language to understand what was happening to me. At that moment it just felt like everyone, including myself, didn't like me or want anything to do with me.

Now that I look back, so many of those experiences were rooted in anti-Blackness and internalized racism, pushing the narrative that I needed to hate being Black. I struggled with this

113

for years, thinking about the ways I critiqued things as "ghetto" or how I never wanted to go to the "Black gay clubs." I never knew it all started with the media I was consuming and how I was being made to feel about myself.

I also realized too that fatphobia was rearing its ugly head, and I had no idea the impact that would have on me as well, considering all that I was learning about being fat came from television and film. Many people in the media had eating disorders, and at one point in history it felt like it was being celebrated. Even now with the Ozempic craze, it reminds me of the times I would see insane diets on magazines and on television shows like *TMZ* and *Inside Edition*.

So many of those experiences made me feel not only ugly but unlovable. It made me feel as if I was the problem in a world that saw Blackness, fatness, and queerness as an issue. I was left constantly wondering "If I can't find people here and I can't find community at school, then where am I wanted?" This brought me back to the early feelings I had of suicide ideation.

What I needed was someone, like a Latrice Royale, to tell me the answer.

■ ■ ■

I always say that everything, and I do mean everything, in my life somehow always comes back to *RuPaul's Drag Race* (*RPDR*). No matter what is going on in my life, I can always think of a moment on the show that will relate. That's why even though I am not the biggest fan of RuPaul and his politics, I can definitely vouch for the importance of the show.

I didn't get into *Drag Race* until I met my partner. I thought it was another television show that was just going to perpetuate queer people as mean and catty, something that I had grown tired of seeing on other reality television competition shows with queer contestants.

After months of trying to ignore the show and its growing fandom, both my partner and some of my friends began hosting *Drag Race* watch parties where we would not only get together and talk about our favorite queens but also throw shade at the drag queens we didn't like.

Not for nothing, I was somewhat apprehensive about even engaging in these conversations because at that time in television, I never felt as if these shows were interested in seeing Black Fat Femmes as people. I often saw them as the ones that everyone had beef with and were often made to be the "angry Black queen" always looking for trouble.

I saw this with season 2 of *RPDR*, specifically with one queen by the name of Mystique who went viral for screaming, "B**ch, I am from Chicago!" I really wanted to root for her, but from the first episode, I could see what producers were doing. The show needed a villain, and Mystique had all the perfect attributes of being one. She was Black, she was fat, and she was a femme queer, and this translated to her being always angry and ready to fight.

Much of what turned me off from watching the show was the ways folks both on-and offline dog piled on Mystique. At the time, I had no idea that any of this was because of inherent bias or anti-Blackness and fatphobia, but I just knew I didn't like the way it made me feel.

Every week I began to see Mystique be painted as an evil clown on the show, but by the time she was sent packing on the show, I felt like she was just another punching bag for (white) queer people to spit on. I also kept asking myself why it felt like they kept painting Mystique out to be angry every episode when, in reality, so much of what she was experiencing was exactly what I had experienced in queer spaces. The constant feeling of being poked, prodded, and judged immediately and seeing white queer individuals get away with how they continued to treat her.

The same would happen in season 3 with Stacy Layne Matthews, where the show painted her out to be a chicken-eating Black Fat Femme with a "poor attitude." What bothered me so much was knowing that Stacy felt this and watching other non-Black queens on the show call her a "booger" because she wasn't as polished or celebrated by the *RPDR* judges.

By the end of season 3, I was practically done with the franchise. I wanted nothing to do with the show because I was tired of seeing Black Fat Femmes be treated like trash by other non-Black queens on the show and no one calling it out or naming it. I was also bothered that no one on the show defended her and that no one in my immediate group saw it the way I did.

When season 4 was announced, I truly paid it dust. While everyone in my circle who watched the show was super excited for its return, I continued to scream from the hilltops that Black Fat Femmes were only put on the show so that they could be a punching bag. Even now with all the show's critical acclaim and success, I still believe that Black queens don't get a fair shot on the show, and one day I might write a book about that.

Reflecting on it now, I wish I could go back in time and tell both Mystique and Stacy Layne Matthews how sorry I am for what they experienced on the show and why their time on the show was not only important to me and other Black Fat Femmes but also woke up my intersectional politics around the Black Fat Femme experience.

By the time season 4 was actually on the air, I was pretty much on my phone waiting to blow up social media about the spectacle I was going to see around Latrice Royale. I had seen what *RPDR* had done more times than I needed to. I was out of grace and ready to fight for my sister. I wasn't going to sit quietly through another season where another Black Fat Femme would be treated poorly on the show, and I recall myself being very vocal about it on social media.

Considering I didn't have the social media following then that I currently have, most days I felt like I was screaming into the void. In my mind, I was just another Black Fat Femme screaming about the ways we are portrayed and treated unfairly in the media all to be gaslit by friends and fans of the show who thought *I* was the problem.

What I wanted more than anything was to let Latrice know that I saw her and was doing anything and everything on my end to support her so she wouldn't fall prey to what Mystique had gone through in her season. Now, it was extremely presumptuous to think Latrice needed my help, but that is how much I loved her. I saw something in her, almost like learning my blood relative was going on the show, and I was going to use what little platform I had to protect her because that's how much her visibility on the show meant to me.

Latrice, though, seemed to have a pretty good understanding of how seasons 2 and 3 went and made it really clear that in her season she wasn't going to let the producers or the fans of the show make her out to be a fool. This spoke to me because up until this moment I had never seen a queen, specifically a Black queen, immediately demand so much space and respect.

In particular, after the Snatch Game episode (where *Drag Race* contestants pretend to be other celebrities), she shared so much about her life that reminded me of my own experience:

growing up in Compton, spending most of her life feeling like she would never be able to find success because of the intersections of her identity.

It changed my life because I had never seen a Black Fat Femme take their craft so seriously, but more, it was a night-and-day difference from season 2 where Mystique seemed scorned by the experiences she had not just on the show but in life.

Latrice had something to say. Latrice had work to do. Latrice was reminding everyone that not only was she chunky yet funky but that she was there to make history on the show, and that is exactly what she did.

What is more iconic than anything when it comes to my standom of Latrice Royale is not only how she carried herself on the show but that you could hear and see the intentionality and thought behind every word and action she had. It's not lost on me that Latrice was Aretha Franklin in her season of Snatch Game, and both on and off the show, she wanted one thing:

R.E.S.P.E.C.T.

Up to this point, I never knew I had the autonomy to demand respect from anyone, specifically non-Black queer people. For years, I was so used to them passively saying mean things to me and about me because of who I was that I just accepted that it would always be that way.

But Latrice helped me to understand that just because people think they can doesn't mean they should.

Latrice Royale wanted the other queens to respect not only her presence but all that she had been through to get to that point in her life. She had been through both the fire and

118

trenches in her life as a Black Fat Femme, and she was letting the world know that she had the right to not just exist, but she was showing everyone what it looked like to thrive.

I was so moved by it, I immediately told myself that I had to meet her and tell her to her face how much her time on the show impacted me. I needed to tell her how thankful I was to see her and know that she existed and to thank her for being so forward about all the things she had gone through to remind me that my struggle in life would not be in vain.

Later that year I went to see her perform at a show in the Inland Empire, but there was so much pandemonium around her that I didn't get a real chance to fully sit down and tell her the impact her time on the show had on my life.

That's why when DragCon was announced in 2015, I ran to Los Angeles quicker than I ever have to be first in her line. I remember seeing her and her welcoming me in with open arms. What made the moment even more special was that she knew me and had seen some of my tweets around how much she impacted me and my life. When she hugged me, I burst into tears and thanked her for telling me that I had the right to be unapologetically Black Fat Femme.

She also told me that I can't wait for folks to honor me – that I have to demand it. This was something no one had ever told me. Ugly Oprah crying for sure.

While I could go on for chapters about that moment and how validating it was for me, it reminded me that there *were* possibility models out there for me to look up to. Even though I didn't know her or her walk, she saw me in mine and we saw each other.

She spent years battling systems that tried to take our light away, and in that moment, Latrice gave it back to me. Not only did she hand it to me, but she told me to hold it and to demand more if someone doesn't want to give it to me.

To this day, I still don't think I have ever told her how much that moment meant and, without it, how I might not have been here to write about it.

Latrice Royale (left) and me at RuPaul's DragCon in Los Angeles, California, 2015

Chapter 6

To Be Loved

"Some men like a man with a little sugar in their tank!"
—Rodney Chester as "Alex" in *Noah's Arc*

I can't tell you the first time I ever felt ugly. I just knew, by societal standards, I was. It was something that I always felt in the depths of my soul and there was nothing that anyone could do to change it.

Ugly was a state of being for me, and it often made me feel like no one was ever going to love me.

A lot of it was internal. But, life also had its messed-up ways of reminding me that I wasn't "the attractive one."

Much of it began with me being teased relentlessly in grammar school not just for the ways in which I performed masculinity but for the ways I looked and dressed. Between my big thick coke bottle glasses, my oddly shaped head, face and haircuts, and being sweaty because of how big I was, people made sure to remind me that I was the "weird" kid. Time and time again.

To make matters worse, my brother and I would often share the same clothes (and the kids at our school were quick to clock it), thus me getting teased even more for being both poor and fat. It was the perfect equation to make me super self-conscious. Even now, I catch myself thinking "I don't want to look poor" when going to do something because I can still hear my peers in my head teasing me for how I looked.

Most of my embarrassment came from the moments that I realized that I was a true "fat kid." On the first day of school when kids were in class looking for their friends to sit next to, I had to sit at a desk that had a detached seat because I could not fit in a regular seat. This meant I sat at the desk next to the teacher's desk. The "fat kid table."

Having a really bad skin condition (eczema, which I later learned was dermatitis) that made my skin flare up in really bad hives only added to the surmounting teasing I got.

This led me to believe that somehow I deserved all of the mean and nasty things people said and did to me because "That is just how the world is." I just learned to accept it. I began to expect that people would say and be mean to me not just for how I looked but also for me being queer, and I started to believe that all the things I was enduring – how I looked, my skin, and even my identity – was a punishment from God.

I often would spend my days alone asking God, "Why me?" I didn't realize how much of what I was experiencing was having a huge impact on my mental health. For years, I really wanted to end my life because I began to feel like my family's love wasn't enough. And I still live with the ideations to this day because of my lived experiences.

By the time I was 14, I was seeing a school therapist every week, checking in about my mental health. The major concern was that I was thinking about how I would end my life – but no one had the words to help me feel better at the time. No one was discussing intersectionality and the ways oppression was making me feel. No one understood that so much of the poverty and oppression I was experiencing as a young Black queer kid was impacting my want to live. I kept thinking, "It's always gonna be this bad, and I simply don't want to have to endure it."

Even in the moments where I started to grow out of my skin condition and find people who seemed to accept me as a young queer child, I had been taught by the world that the color of my skin, my size, and my identity would always be a problem. Even with coming to terms that there was nothing I could do about my skin condition, I still hated my size, and I hated how I was treated because of it. This led me to feeling like I always needed to wear long sleeves and pants because both my skin and my size made me so uncomfortable.

"What's wrong with your skin? Why are you so fat?"

The long sleeves and baggy pants became my armor. Black long sleeves and baggy pants, to be precise, in 110° San Bernardino, California, heat? In my mind, I would rather die than be caught wearing shorts and have someone question me about how my skin looked the way it did.

As time went on, it got harder to hide my body. Around 16, I began to feel the pressure to show it off more – not because I wanted to but because people around me pressured me to. My cousins would walk around shirtless all the time, and when I didn't, they would often poke fun at me and laugh. "Look at his titties!" some of my cousins would say. "Jon has titties like a girl!" For years, I thought to myself, "If I ever get enough money, the first thing I will do is get gynecomastia removal/my chest fixed."

I hated the thought of the world thinking I had breasts like a woman because I was already being teased for being effeminate. Now, at the age where I was supposed to look more "manly," I was being teased for something else that is out of my control.

Great.

By the time I was old enough to conceptualize what it meant to be me in the LGBTQ+ community, I was so down on myself and the way I felt about my looks because I knew that there was nothing I could ever really do to *be* conventionally attractive. When you constantly grow up being teased for being ugly and then you hear, "no Blacks, no Fats, no Femmes" – and you realize you've grown up to be everything the world hates – it feels like you really should just give up.

So I came up with the plan. By 17, I'm outta here.

In the meantime, while I was thinking about how I planned to unalive myself, I ate. And I ate some more, and when I began making my own money from working my part-time job at Wendy's, my portions only got bigger. I figured, "The world will never love me or see me as beautiful at this size, so I might as well continue to indulge the one thing that has never been mean to me."

While my hatred for my body continued to grow, so did my size *and* my love of food.

My family began to notice because I gained almost 50 pounds over the span of 6 months. But, my health was never a major concern; "Being fat won't get you any girls" was. My uncles were more concerned with me having a girlfriend than actually asking me why I was eating everything in sight. Honestly, it wasn't even the teasing about my size or my identity that was the worst. It was how fixated all my uncles and male cousins were on how many girls I had on my roster and, in the words of one uncle, "how many hoes I was having sex with."

My uncle's favorite thing to say to me? "If you lose weight, you'll be able to take your shirt off at the pool." Why? Because this was the time I should be showing off to get the attention of girls. This, all while my cousins who played football would throw jabs at me about my lack of interest both in sports and in women while questioning my sexuality.

Hypermasculinity was almost worse than homophobia. Almost. I was scared, and I didn't know what else to do but eat.

Considering that all my male cousins began to bulk up instead of gaining weight like I did at that age (and show off more of their bodies because they felt like they had something to prove), I kept doing anything and everything that I could to hide mine. However, when I reached a size 4XL, it became harder to find things to wear, which then led me to wearing the same things over and over again. This threw me right back into the vicious cycle of being teased, which then – you guessed it – only caused me to eat even more.

By this time, considering that I felt like no one in this world would ever find me attractive or love me, food became the thing I was in a relationship with. It became my source of joy. It was the only thing that never rejected me or made me hate who I truly was.

Except, until it did.

It was like I couldn't stop overeating. It only got worse when I got a summer job and started realizing how easy it was for me to get food. Junk food became the big hug I was waiting to have.

"Whew, you're getting big, my boy," my family would often say. Or, that if I kept eating, my mother would have to get another job. Everything they said only made me that much hungrier.

The growing hatred I began to develop for my body began to suffocate me. I noticed how people looked at me when I tried to run on the track at school. I can remember my cross country teacher asking me if I wanted to run just a little bit further and hearing folks on the team laugh, saying "I needed it."

By the time I was old enough to understand that I *might* have had an eating disorder, I was already in a full-blown polyamorous relationship with Chef Boyardee and Häagen-Dazs.

But it wasn't just my body that I grew to hate. I always hated my soft facial features. Though I know most of the self-hatred was rooted in what I now know as femmephobia, I think much of it was internalized misogynoir – the hatred for Black women.

From a young age, I was always told I looked like my mother. My facial features and expressions were always likened to her, and while I think she is the most beautiful woman in the world, I hated the thought of looking like a woman. People would always say, "You look just like your mom," and I knew what they were saying. I looked too much like a woman.

The thing was, I knew it wasn't positive. I was often defending myself from something someone had said or done to me – what I now know as abusive. Or, it was said in moments where I felt like I was being policed for *how* I performed. I never felt like being likened to my mother was a slight until I got old enough to understand that acting like a woman was, in fact, a problem.

Hearing this over and over again from family sparked the deep-seated hatred I had for my looks. For much of my adolescent years, you couldn't get me to look in a mirror or me to take a photo. It was like I was a vampire, and the thought of me seeing my reflection or someone taking a photo of me would cause me to melt away.

I hated everything about me, including the things that reminded me of the woman I loved so much.

For years, I would stand in the mirror and poke at my face thinking to myself that one day I would have enough money to get surgery on my face to make it more masculine. I would get chiseled cheeks and a broader chin. At one point, I began saving all of the money I was making from my first job in a piggy bank thinking that one day I would be able to afford enough money so that I can start researching facial reconstruction surgery.

I even thought about asking my primary-care doctor about putting me on testosterone so that my features (and my voice) could become more masculine. I was desperate to appear more manly, and I was willing to do anything to get there, even if I had to pay for it or put my life at risk for it.

I would often wake up early just to go to the school library to use the library computers and scroll through all the photos of celebrities I wanted to look like. I then would go to the Web and search the insane ways that celebrities were keeping themselves thin while also looking for ways to make myself more attractive on a budget. I was desperate and was willing to do practically anything to make myself feel better about how much I hated myself.

But the obsession with looking different only grew worse with time. So much that I never looked at myself long enough in the mirror. If I did catch a glimpse of myself in the mirror, it would ruin my day. It was easy for me to hate me because I knew the world hated me, and I was reminded of it every day I stepped outside into it.

But then came the times in my formative years where everyone around me had someone who had an interest in them, and again I was still the only person without a crush who liked them back. I would sit in the back of class watching boys and girls go back and forth passing notes and blowing kisses at each other. I was in the Gay Straight Alliance at school and often watched guys and girls come to the meetings hand and hand, wondering if and when love would find me.

More than anything, I kept thinking "What's wrong with me that no one seemed remotely interested or attracted to me?"

Love was something in my head that I always wanted. Love was something that I spent so many years of my life being fixated on because the media told me that if I didn't have people, specifically other queer men falling all over me, my worth would in fact be worthless.

Love was so tangible to me, but it was something that I could never reach or touch.

When I got to college, the feeling and deep desire to want someone to "love me" almost became uncontrollable. I scoured all sides of the Internet with hopes that I would find someone to validate me and the (lack) of love I had for myself. I spent hours and hours talking to men online with the thought that if I could find someone to just love me, it would make my world so much more bearable.

Now reflecting on it, so much of it was connected to the feelings of isolation I had growing up as a Black Fat Femme and the feelings of loneliness that come with being the only Black queer person in so many small spaces.

For so much of my life, I saw love as something that would accidentally happen to me, and then I would have a cute story to tell, like all the white queer friends I knew both in high school and college when it came to my love story.

But that never happened.

When I joined XY.com, I was told, "You're not my type." When I was on Gay.com and Myspace.com, I was told, "You're not my type." To other (queer) men, I was just a type, not a person – and that wore on me. It hurt to know that all anyone ever saw was my appearance and how I presented myself.

By the time I was old enough to understand *why* I hated myself after the culmination of years of internalized and externalized hatred, I felt like no one was ever going to love me. Even when I mentioned the feeling to my mother and therapist, I was met with "You're young. Love will come."

But even at my young age, there was this deep-rooted feeling that because of how I looked and because of who I was, no one would ever love me. I figured, if I can't even like me, who will ever love me?

■ ■ ■

Whenever I am asked, "What else do you think aided in a lot of your self-hatred?" I immediately tell people to go back to the early 2000s, specifically television and film. Beyond the lack of positive representation of Black Fat Femmes, the messaging to be thin was everywhere. You couldn't be in a classroom without hearing someone tell you that eating vegetables would make you skinny. You couldn't open a magazine without reading about some miracle diet that some skinny white celebrity was on. Media basically beat it over your head that if you were anything other than white or skinny, you were ugly.

Growing up in the early 2000s meant navigating a cultural landscape heavily influenced by the media's narrow definitions of beauty and desirability with subtle reminders that those who looked "different" were undeserving of both love and, more importantly, respect. Then came the pressure to conform to societal ideals, particularly the messaging concerning appearance. Many of the messages I received as a child about my looks were unrelenting to a point where now I spend much of my time with my therapist unpacking the terrible messages I got about my looks from early 2000s media.

From early 2000 to late 2010, media outlets – film, television, and magazines – were fixated on promoting a homogeneous standard of beauty while also implying that being "different" (Black Fat Femme) made you an outlier. Advertisements bombarded screens with images of slim, white male and female celebrities endorsing countless weight-loss products, reinforcing the message that thinness equated to success and attractiveness. The idea that someone like Luther Vandross could be successful while fat was an anomaly, something that he often spoke out about during his time alive.

The portrayal of celebrities like Anna Nicole Smith epitomized this obsession: her weight fluctuations were scrutinized publicly, with her return to fame seemingly contingent upon achieving a slimmer figure as the face of TrimSpa.

The narrative extended beyond celebrities to influential figures like Oprah Winfrey and Tyra Banks, who publicly battled with their weight under the relentless gaze of the media, as both of them very publicly spoke out about media obsessions with looks. Oprah's candid discussions about her struggles with weight were televised spectacles, highlighting how even the most successful and admired individuals were not immune to societal pressures. Tyra Banks defiantly confronted critics who commented on her weight gain, underscoring the pervasive body shaming prevalent in media culture and leading her to scream, "Kiss my fat ass!" on public television.

Remember platforms like "Hot or Not" and Perez Hilton's blog? The kicker was that he himself was struggling with his own weight loss and was putting down other celebrities for not matching the ideal. The nerve.

It was almost like people enjoyed seeing people get shamed for how they looked. These sites not only perpetuated narrow standards of beauty and desirability, but they also reminded you how undesirable you were if you were a Black Fat Femme.

These sites not only reinforced the preference for thinness but also often emphasized whiteness as a benchmark of attractiveness. For those who did not fit these criteria, the implication was clear: they fell short of societal standards of beauty.

Retail stores were also no exception. Stores like Hollister and Abercrombie & Fitch epitomized the "cool" aesthetic of the early 2000s, catering primarily to a narrow demographic that matched their idealized image of youth and conventional attractiveness. For many, shopping in these stores became a stark reminder of how their appearance diverged from what was considered "hot" by mainstream media.

The impact of these messages was compounded by the rise of social media, specifically the rise of "social media influencers" who too were being critiqued for their looks. The emergence of platforms like Myspace and later Facebook introduced new arenas for comparison and self-evaluation – constantly causing me to try to figure out how to leverage the platform to make me "attractive" enough to garner a relationship. Social media began to establish the norms, perpetuating an environment where popularity and self-worth were often tied to physical appearance and social validation.

Media made everyone self-conscious in the early 2000s, and the growth of social media has only made it worse.

For individuals from marginalized communities, particularly Black people, the lack of representation in mainstream media further exacerbated feelings of inadequacy. Shows like *Queer as Folk* and *Will & Grace*, while groundbreaking in their portrayal of LGBTQ+ characters, predominantly featured white actors, perpetuating a limited and exclusionary view of beauty and desirability. Even when token efforts were made to diversify casts, such as adding Taye Diggs to *Will & Grace*, it often felt more like a token gesture than genuine inclusivity.

Nothing felt genuine about that season, and even thinking about it now, I cringe.

The cumulative effect of these influences was profound. I can say that part of my insecurities began with internalizing the messages that my worth was contingent upon conforming to unattainable standards of beauty perpetuated by the media, specifically on social media. This led me to a pervasive sense of insecurity and self-doubt, particularly among those whose appearances diverged from the normative ideal.

The pervasive influence of media, coupled with the emergence of social media, reinforced narrow ideals of attractiveness and perpetuated unrealistic expectations of myself, causing me to feel like I needed to be perfect, not only to exist but in order to find real love.

■ ■ ■

By the time I got to college, I accepted that I was a Black Fat Femme who would never find love all because of the way I looked. I had tried dating and had even started going to clubs to try to expand my LGBTQ+ circle. I was still having a hard time with my identity and didn't really know what to make of my life now that I was officially out.

I was still very hopeful that one day someone would sweep me off my feet and change how I felt not only about myself but about love in general. The challenge I kept finding was that so many of the queer men I had met felt the same way I did, and what are two hopeless people going to do in a relationship?

For months, I worked with a college therapist who helped me understand that a lot of the feelings I had about myself (and love) stemmed from many of the experiences I had growing up and reminded me that life wouldn't always be that way.

As time went on and I began to meet other LGBTQ+ people in college, I quickly realized that many of them were also turning to the media to find a positive representation of not just queer people but queer love. In one of my classes, I was challenged by a professor to do exactly this, and after asking around, someone put me on to a show that has probably had the biggest impact on not just how I see myself but also my outlook on love.

"Have you ever watched *Noah's Arc?*" someone asked me in passing.

"No," I replied.

"You actually remind me of one of the characters on that show. His name is Alex."

I was beyond intrigued.

Now, it wasn't that I had no idea that the show existed, because one of my best friends in my last year of high school was really into the show at the time. Considering we only ever had basic cable in my room (meaning that I didn't get premium channels like Showtime, Cinemax, or Logo), I had no real context of what the show was about.

I just knew it was a gay show, and I had already gotten in trouble for trying to watch other queer-themed shows in my home in the past and wasn't trying to add more fuel to the fire.

So, when I got to college and had a chance to buy my own DVD player, the first box set I purchased was *Noah's Arc*.

For those who might not be familiar with the show, much of it centers around a character named Noah (played by Darryl Stephens) and his struggles with dating and finding love in Los Angeles, California. It also involves many other characters who, like Noah, are Black queer men. While the show, created by Black queer writer Patrik-Ian Polk, centers on many of the experiences Black queer men deal with around love and sex, the show had one character that not only validated parts of my identity but also showed me that love was in fact possible.

While I, too, found myself agreeing with Noah in parts of his journey, Alex (played by Rodney Chester), was a big deal for me, not just because of him being a Black Fat Femme but because he was me. He was flamboyant. He spoke his mind. He had no problem with letting others know how he felt about things.

One of the things I loved most about the show was that Alex felt like a whole person. I had gotten so used to watching shows and expecting Black Fat Femmes to be the sidekick, but this was the first time I had ever seen a character like Alex be a whole person. Seeing a character not only be liked but be loved at this time really changed my perspective on life (and is really what made me want to work in entertainment in the first place).

Rodney's character was also extremely passionate, not just about his HIV clinic but about his partner, Trey (played by Gregory Kieth). This blew me away, because I had been told time and time again that I wore my heart on my sleeve and that doing so would in turn cause me a lot of heartache in life.

To see a character love hard and *be* loved hard reminded me of how deserving I was of my "Trey" and how I didn't have to settle for less just because the world kept telling me that, as a Black Fat Femme, "less" is what I deserved.

While there were several storylines around Alex and Trey's love, one of the things I took from watching the show was that everyone saw Alex as a beacon of light and hope. Watching Alex's growth throughout the show, along with the struggles he too had around his identity, allowed me to feel human in a way that I had never felt before.

In addition, it was watching Trey show Alex that he was deserving of love that really changed my mind on how I felt about the love I felt like I would never have. It was the first time I had received the message – from anywhere – that I too could be loved by someone in the way Trey loved Alex.

The best parts of the show were also the moments in which we saw Alex struggling with parts of his identity and how it almost felt like other characters normalized the struggle. It also reminded the viewers – like me – that we are so much more than our struggles. Seeing Alex living a life and thriving while overcoming the struggles reminded me that I had a right to not only exist but be in love *while* existing.

This was powerful, and I have yet to find another show that has given me that message. *Noah's Arc* was truly my saving grace. As Alex would often say to all of his peers in the show, "Some men really do like a man with sugar in their tank."

■ ■ ■

One of the things I was told constantly while dating was that I needed to "love myself before I could love anyone else." I heard so many people say it – hell, RuPaul has built a whole show around that idea and concept. But I'd be remiss if I didn't mention how dangerous that concept is, especially for Black Fat Femmes who like me struggle to find love.

Not just love from a significant other, but from someone else in the LGBTQ+ community. Reflecting on the character Alex, it would be easy to make the assumption that the reason Trey would love him is because he did the work to love himself. But no one ever really thinks about how hard it is for Black Fat Femmes to love themselves when they are constantly getting the message – both from the straight world and the queer world – that they are unlovable.

This was something that I had battled for years until I met my partner – thinking that because I didn't "love myself enough" that it was the reason that I couldn't find love. But the truth of the matter is that the world doesn't make it easy for Black Fat Femmes to love themselves. It doesn't make it easy for us to *be* loved.

So many of the things I hated about myself were things I had to unlearn. My skin color, my performance, and my size are not dictators of how much love I should (or shouldn't) be given from the world. Moreover, I also had to learn that knowing how much the world despised me and how much I would be reminded of that day in and day out, it was my duty to remind not only myself but others who I brought into my life on how to treat me.

That is truly what I learned from watching Alex on *Noah's Arc*. I have the right and the duty in my life to remind others about how they should treat me and love me. That life was about reclaiming my power not just in my day to day, but also in my love life.

While there are countless dating stories that I could share about the ways in which cisgender queer men treated me like I was just a sexual object, the reality is that I *let* them treat me that way. I believed that because I was a Black Fat Femme who was used to getting the scraps in life, I deserved to get the scraps in love too.

Alex taught me that this was a lie that Black Fat Femmes are fed.

Seeing Rodney Chester embody a character who not only loved themselves but told the world *how* to love them taught me how to love myself. More than anything, both Rodney and Alex told me that I couldn't just wait for the world to love me. I had to demand it.

That is truly what self-love is. It's not just saying, "I love myself" and letting that be it. It's about telling the world how to love you. It's about also stomping out all the awful ways the world makes you feel like you just have to accept what is given to you.

If anyone should take anything away from this chapter, it's the importance of knowing that self-love isn't just about saying "I like/love myself." It's loudly letting both the world (and cis queer men) know that because of all that you have endured, you're not just going to be treated in any kind of way.

It's knowing what makes you feel good. It's vocalizing what doesn't and recognizing that if it doesn't make *you* happy, you have the right to walk away from it. It's also a reminder that you have the right to have the kind of love *you* feel you merit.

Because you indeed deserve to be loved.

Chapter 7

Becoming That B*tch

"Walk like it's for sale and rent is due tonight!"

—Miss J

I almost titled this chapter "Conversations with a Therapist," but I stuck with "Becoming That B*tch" because that's exactly what my therapist helped me with.

I've been working with my therapist for almost seven years, and she is the reason I was able to understand what it means to become "that b*tch." Yes, there was a lot of crying and sighing in her office, but most of the work came from me recognizing that I as a Black Fat Femme deserved to not just love myself, but that I had the right to make my life what I wanted.

Up to the point I had met her, most of my life was spent with me fighting to exist. One day, she kindly asked me as I entered our session, "Why are you always ready to jump into the ring? When are you gonna be the person that runs the fight?"

It was in that moment she literally changed my life.

Now keep in mind, I didn't get a good therapist until my late 30s because the truth of the matter is that a lot of therapists don't know how to navigate the needs of Black Fat Femmes. There was a time in my life where I was switching therapists out of my life like Destiny's Child members.

After going through multiple therapists who gaslit me, filled the room with anti-Blackness, or were covertly (and sometimes overtly) homophobic, I finally found a therapist who got me. She made it very clear to me that she wouldn't be able to solve all my problems (which I never really expected her to), but she did say that her job was to offer me resources that could make my life better.

She did exactly that.

One of the things we spent a lot of time talking about in our first years together was my obsession with perfection. More specifically, my obsession with trying to live up to the expectations of white cisgender people.

One day in one of our sessions, she noted, "It sounds like you weren't ugly. It sounds like you just grew up around too many white people."

My mouth dropped. It was like for the first time, I had someone really take a piece of how I have always felt and vocalize it in a way that I can wholeheartedly comprehend. It was like for the first time I had met someone who saw how and where my self-hatred began and helped me walk through the emotions of unpacking them.

Now, I want to be clear that I don't think I am ugly, nor do I believe that I have ever been ugly. However, life made me believe that I was, because in our world, there is only one standard of beauty.

Skinny. Cisgender. White.

Note: I do want to make it clear that me saying this is not me bashing white queer people; it's about understanding the ways in which white supremacy showed up in my life and how it manifests on a systemic level.

One of the biggest things I realized was that a lot of the messaging I got in my younger years was that I wasn't "attractive" or "good enough" because of how I presented. However, when you decide to blossom even in the worst soil, folks wonder how that is even possible. Hell, I sometimes wondered that too.

Up until this point in my life I had never been challenged to think that maybe I wasn't the problem and that everyone around me had an issue because of how confident I read. My therapist would tell me time and time again about how the oppressor (often queer cisgender white men) are worried you might see the cracks in their castles, which is why they move and operate in the ways that they do.

Beyond our conversation about internalized racism, fatphobia, and femmephobia, we got into deep conversations about how the process to your bad b*tchery starts with having to re-introduce you, to *you*.

When she began to list all of the things I accomplished and had overcome in my life, it dawned on me that I might just be *that girl*. I had truly always been that girl, but I never fully owned it because I wasn't giving myself the agency to do so and life wasn't giving me the chance to do it either.

I had become used to lemons being squirted in my wounds, and all I could look for was pain. But what I have learned both in and out of therapy is that after a while, you realize that you can only cry so long about the pain before you have to do something to end it.

To be clear, I am not saying by any means that we deserve the pain we endure or that we are the only masters of ending it. Truthfully, we deserve so much more because of what we go through as Black Fat Femmes.

However, what we know about our experiences and how the world treats us is a reminder for how we have never been built to break, and that is what makes us so much stronger. In the words of my beautiful mother, "Sometimes you gotta go through some stuff to get to the good stuff," and that's exactly what my life (and this book) truly is about.

Something someone said to me in my 20s that really shaped my world was that life gives you two options: either you stay in said mess and drown, or you can use it to help you grow. Kinda like a flower.

So many of us know this about ourselves. We are the seeds that the world never knew they planted. We have continued to grow and find foundations within ourselves, often making the oppressor angry that we won't just "go away." Like actress Jenifer Lewis once said, "If you sit in sh** for too long, it stops smelling."

Let's sit with that for a bit because I know that so many of us feel like there isn't anything good that can come out of owning our identity as a Black Fat Femme. While I don't want to get too preachy, I want us to understand that we don't have to always accept the bad that is handed to us. It's about demanding the respect that you give so freely to everyone else. It's also about recognizing the power in being a Black Fat Femme. You've had it in you all along. So did our ancestors and trans and nonbinary siblings.

We have been and will always be the blueprint.

Even with all the moments of sadness and self-doubt that I had, it hit me that there were way too many people both in my life and in the media that were showing me the way to become that b*tch. I had the power to own all elements of my identity, and the world (and others) could look at my experiences as something they could use to learn from.

I recognized early on in my younger years that life had handed me a whole deck of yellow Uno cards and told me to play. No Draw Fours. No Reverses or Skips. Just a whole deck of yellow number cards. After years of asking "Why me?" and being mad about the ways life seemed to forget about me, I woke up one morning and said, "This isn't always going to be my life" and that I had to be the one to change the way I felt about me *AND* my life.

When I was going into my late 20s, I kept thinking to myself "It can't always be rain." André, Miss Lawrence, Latrice Royale, and so many other Black Fat Femmes were the teachers, and instead of trying to figure it out on my own, I decided to let them light my path.

After years of feeling like being a Black Fat Femme was a curse, I finally had to sit myself down and have a little heart to heart. Much of it came from the many meltdowns and panic attacks I kept having. I knew that this wasn't the life I wanted to live.

I decided to stop looking at the color of the cards and decided that I needed to figure out how I was going to play my hand. That was the message that the universe was giving me. It's not what you have, it's how you play.

The greater message in all of this was figuring out how to beat oppression at its own game. Considering I thought I was doing everything I could to overcome, I quickly learned that "overcoming" wouldn't be enough. I had to live on my own terms, and that is exactly what it has been and honestly always will be: a game that you have to learn how to win for yourself.

My self (and my therapist) kept asking me the same question: What would it take for me to be happy? What would it take for me to stop waiting for the world to approve of me and love me radically?

Up to this point, I had never heard of the concept of "radical self-love" or understood that something like this existed. Hell, I didn't even understand what self-love was let alone the concept of it being radical.

My therapist would later share this with me during one of our last meetings: "Radical self-love is taking care of yourself. It's not just knowing that you have the right to be loved, but more; it's letting go of the idea that you have to be perfect in order to have the love you think you deserve."

My therapist further explained that living proudly as Black, protecting my emotions as a fat person, and caring for my femme (queer) energy was an act of self-preservation. Yes, while I was doing my doctorate at that time, I had heard other scholars like Audre Lorde and James Baldwin talk about it, but I had never had anyone – specifically another Black person – explain to me that being me was in fact, a radical act.

I had never had anyone put it that way to me. I had never had anyone tell me that because I was who I am, the world would always see my lived existence as radical. This really helped me to put things into perspective.

Now, knowing and understanding this, my true work could begin.

Later, my therapist would go on to ask me who is someone that I know, whether personally or not, that could help me in the process of owning my pizzazz. This was something that people always said I had, but I never fully believed it because I felt like life tried to beat it out of me.

You know that feeling. The feeling of waking up so happy about who you are and by the end of the day wondering "Why do I continue to wake up every day?" I quickly realized that a lot of the way I felt about myself was me internalizing the projection of others.

Them trying to knock me down became a way for them to make themselves feel better about the things that they lack or hate about themselves. My therapist has helped me to understand that often people can't harness their personal power and often look to steal it from those who have. That's why the world is so awful to Black Fat Femmes.

In the same conversation, my therapist went on to ask, "Ain't nobody that you know who walks into a room and you think, 'I wanna be like that person when I grow up'?" half-jokingly. The first and *only* person that came to mind was Miss J.

Yes, the grand diva herself, darling.

Up until that point, I had never thought about how much power I could have in my own life by harnessing the energy and emotion that Miss J radiated. Honestly, as much as I saw Miss J growing up, I had never really thought about the impact that she would have on me.

For years, I watched *America's Next Top Model*, eyeing and being in awe of André Leon Talley for the Black fat representation he had offered me. But right there was another icon who, like Andre, was giving me the life lessons that I knew I needed. And while it was something I wish I would have reflected on sooner, I am so glad I had a therapist to help me get it.

■ ■ ■

It would be silly of me to assume that I know Miss J or what the story of their life entails. While much of Miss J's background is elusive, the one thing I *do* know is that the world hasn't been kind to folks who look like them.

I can remember the days growing up when I saw people like Miss J and heard the mean things people said to them. How confident they appeared in a world where people wanted a nonbinary person to move more stealthily as if fear to exist should be their only emotion.

But Miss J served as a reminder of what my life could be once I got out of my own way. She wanted the world to know that she was here, queer, Black, a little chubby, and damn proud of it. She reminded me of a cousin I never really got to know who passed away from AIDS when I was younger. They both wanted the world to know that their light was too bright for anyone to put out.

I can only imagine what Miss J had to endure in an industry *and* world where being proud of your skin, size, and identity could cost you your livelihood. How many people said mean things in passing, thinking it was a joke, while Miss J had to let it roll off of her beautiful dark skin in order to pay her bills. How many times might she have cried herself to sleep, like me, because the world was insistent on her shrinking herself in spaces where white, skinny, cisgender queer people got to shine. How many times was she told that she wasn't good enough, and how many times did she have to talk herself up to keep her depression from taking her down.

Watching her every week on *ANTM* was, in fact, a life lesson. It taught me what it means to be your own superfan and how it's essential to the existence of all Black Fat Femme people.

Studying Miss J was a master class in owning the room, in owning one's identity, but more, in taking back all the things that the world said that Black Fat Femmes were told they could never have. She gave me agency to be the version of me, after years of feeling like who I was as a Black Fat Femme wasn't good enough.

Indeed, she was giving me a lesson on "believe it until you achieve it."

Watching her weekly reminded me of how many rooms I had sashayed into, thinking I was the sh*t even when I didn't truly believe it. Even though she didn't know me and

I didn't know her, she was telling me that I had the right to embrace the intersections of my identity with joy.

It was like I could see her watching me and cheering me on. She was telling me that regardless of whether people like or love us, we belong. This was something that I always looked for in life, and that is exactly what she gave me on *ANTM*. She reassured me that by loving who I was and honoring the person I was becoming, I was in fact leaning into the person I was always meant to be.

As I listened to her talk openly about working in fashion as a Black queer person and how tumultuous the industry could be, I was quickly learning that there was nothing I could not do. I had the key to unlock what made me special, and her legacy was just the roadmap to me understanding that.

Seeing her on television reminded me, too, of what I could be in an industry that still has yet to see us fully. It's an industry where beauty is marked not by how much you've endured in this life but by how willing you are to give into its standards.

However, what brought me so much peace is knowing that even on a bad day, you would have never seen Miss J phased by it. Miss J had something to prove even when she didn't – that Black Fat Femmes are important and essential to the growth of everyone. Moreover, that Black Fat Femmes need to take their flowers instead of waiting for the world to give them flowers.

It was in the moments where I watched Miss J help cisgender women find their voice that I found mine. Watching these women walk back and forth on the runway and stand with so much fear in their body, Miss J would remind each of them that they deserved the right to stand with their heads held high. She would tell them whatever fears they had wouldn't take them to where they wanted to go. Fear would hinder them from walking with purpose.

147

But watching Miss J gave me the most important lesson: being that b*tch meant taking no sh*t.

So much of our confidence as Black Fat Femmes has to come from the inside, considering the world would never fully allow me to like (or love) myself without a fight. It was about walking into a room and commanding respect from the oppressor. This was something I had seen Miss J do time and time again on *ANTM* – when she was on a runway or when she was simply advocating to be her authentic self in her day-to-day life.

In the often cutthroat world of fashion, where appearance is paramount and conformity to narrow standards is expected, Miss J stood as a beacon of defiance and empowerment, and that was the thing I was never able to fully take in.

Queer powerhouses like Miss J and so many other queer people who came before them were reminding me that the world would never validate me. The only person who could validate me and my beauty – both inside and out – would be me. While Miss J was challenging the industry's norms and redefined what it meant to be beautiful and confident, she was also reminding me that by doing the same thing, I was now becoming the person that I have always been meant to be.

For Miss J, her influence extended far beyond the superficialities of just fashion. She embodied resilience in the face of adversity and showed that true beauty lies in embracing one's authentic self. As a Black Fat Femme, she not only broke barriers but shattered stereotypes, demonstrating that size, race, and gender identity should never limit one's potential or aspirations.

Her coaching went beyond mere runway technique; it was a transformative experience for those fortunate enough to work with her. Women emerged from their interactions with Miss J not only with refined modeling skills but with a renewed sense of self-worth and empowerment. She instilled in them the belief that their presence mattered, their voices deserved to be heard, and their bodies were worthy of celebration.

In the broader context of societal norms that often marginalize and exclude, Miss J's advocacy for Black Fat Femmes was revolutionary. She demanded visibility and representation in an industry that historically privileged a narrow definition of beauty. By embracing her own identity unapologetically, she paved the way for others to do the same, challenging the industry to expand its definition of inclusivity.

Reflecting on Miss J's impact, I realized that her lessons transcended the runway. They were about reclaiming space and asserting one's worth in a world that too often diminishes it. She taught me and countless others that confidence begins within, rooted in self-acceptance and resilience against societal pressures to conform.

In my own journey, I've encountered similar challenges navigating spaces where my identity as a Black queer person didn't adhere to societal expectations. But watching Miss J allowed me the ability to define my own narrative and to challenge all the stereotypes that sought to confine me. She taught me how to embody confidence that I never knew I had access to, while also encouraging me to find my authentic voice.

Authenticity was something I always struggled with, and seeing her opened my eyes to who and what I could be. Drawing from her and her legacy was a source of inspiration and empowerment. It was truly the light I needed at what I now consider a dark time in my life.

More than anything, Miss J's legacy is one of authenticity and resilience and reminding folks like me that we set our own standards of what is beautiful. Her impact serves as a constant reminder that visibility matters and that every step toward self-acceptance is a step toward dismantling the barriers that limit us.

Miss J's unwavering commitment to authenticity and empowerment has left an indelible mark on the fashion industry and on the lives of those she mentored. She exemplifies the transformative power of self-love and the importance of challenging societal norms to create a more inclusive and affirming world for all. Her legacy continues to inspire us to embrace our uniqueness, stand tall in our truths, and advocate fiercely for our right to be seen and celebrated.

In short, Miss J was giving the middle finger to the systems that keep so many young Black queer men in shackles. She was telling everyone that there was more than one way to show up in the world, something I never was told or even believed.

While I hated that it took me so long to see it, she was telling me that all the things I hated about myself were in fact the prize. So many people hated me and people like her because we were able to move effortlessly in a world that wanted to keep us confined to the "norm."

But more, it would be silly of me just to say that what Miss J had done – not just in her life but in her legacy – was as simple as "she encouraged me to be who I wanted to be."

No. Miss J was breaking a system that told little Black queer boys that they couldn't stand in their light. That "having too much sugar in your tank" was in fact the flavor of life. Something that so many people in this world wished they could actually taste.

But more, she was helping folks like me realize that it's not about what you have; it's about what you do with it. One quote that lives with me is something she said to one of the girls on the runway. Miss J stated, "She can be ugly as the bottom of my shoe, but if you can walk and have confidence *and* look good, that's all that matters. You can turn ugly into beauty."

Miss J was telling me that all the ugly I had faced in my life – both being called ugly and being treated in an ugly way – was now the soil I needed to build a beautiful life. That was the life lesson.

Now, I understand what she was setting out to do. I clearly understood what she was doing, even when she wasn't vocally laying it out for the world to see. She was helping me understand that seeing myself as beautiful wasn't something I needed agency from others to believe. That I could own every part of my identity, struggle, and strife – and still find the strength to say I was, in fact, beautiful.

She was reminding all of us, like many of the queer Black ancestors before, that we deserved to show ourselves the same love that we so willing give away to others. Also, if the world wasn't gonna give us the space (and grace) to love ourselves, we deserved to take it.

Miss J's presence on *ANTM* was more than just a runway coach; she was truly my life coach if you will. Each week, as I watched Miss J mentor contestants on *ANTM*, I witnessed a transformation beyond the runway. Women not only discovered their runway strut but also reclaimed their narrative and self-worth. It was a profound lesson in embracing one's identity and asserting it boldly in any space. Reflecting on Miss J's impact, I realized the depth of her message: true confidence springs from within, nurtured by the understanding that our value isn't defined by external validation but by our own self-perception.

For years, I was so stuck on the idea that because I didn't look like everyone else, I was somehow the problem. But Miss J taught me that being like the other white queer men that the world finds "attractive" wouldn't allow me to have a story to own or, frankly, a book to write. That it wouldn't give me an opportunity to tell other Black Fat Femmes that they have the right to speak openly and honestly about their journey.

What I learned from her and will always take from watching her is that part of the mastery of being a Black Fat Femme is taking what the world calls ugly and making it beautiful.

In further conversations with my therapist after I had time to reflect on this, I began to unravel the layers of significance that Miss J presented. She embodied the struggle and triumph of Black Fat Femmes, navigating a world that often overlooked or undermined their existence. Her journey on *ANTM* wasn't just about modeling; it was about reclaiming space, celebrating resilience, and challenging societal norms that sought to diminish her worth. Through her words and actions, she conveyed a powerful truth: that beauty, confidence, and strength come in diverse forms, each deserving of recognition and respect.

As I think about Miss J's influence, it's one that transcends the boundaries of reality television. It's one that reminds all Black Fat Femmes that we shouldn't sell ourselves short. If anything, it's a reminder of how powerful we really are and how our likeness is a superpower that very few people will ever understand.

Miss J's words, courage, and legacy remain a guiding light for those who dare to defy norms, embrace their uniqueness, and forge their path with unapologetic confidence. Her legacy continues to inspire a generation to walk into any room, runway, or challenge with the assurance that their presence matters and their story deserves to be told.

Plus, she reminds me that I ain't gotta do nothing but be Black Fat Femme and fabulous and die.

And that's law.

■ ■ ■

Reflecting on the talents and lived experiences of folks like Miss J has taught me that Black Fat Femmes are so much more worthy than what we give ourselves credit for.

It took me a long time to get to a place where I could look both inside and outside of myself and say I love the person I've become. It wasn't easy to get here, *but damn it, I've arrived.* While most will tell you to relish in the journey to becoming the person you are, I would say that you have the right to enjoy both the person you've been and the person you've become because there is so much you can learn from both of them.

One of the things I have learned is how much resentment I have held in my body for the person I once was and the decisions I made. But as I've gotten older and have been able to do my own healing, I have learned so much about forgiveness, not just for those who have wronged me but for myself.

It's not lost on me that folks didn't know what to do with me. Just like I was never given a manual to loving me as a Black Fat Femme, others didn't have one either. I am not making excuses for the hurt; I am just saying that while I want to offer grace to myself, I can offer grace to others as well.

As a Black Fat Femme, I have a habit of holding on to hurt and using it as ammo in times I'm harmed, but I have learned how painful (and dangerous) that can be. Learning to let go of the things that not only hurt me but also the ways I've hurt myself has given me a sense of peace that I never knew I could have.

More, it has made me see the younger me as someone who – like my family/peers – was doing the best they could with what little they had. When I was able to see things from that perspective, it really changed the way I loved on me. It changed the way I loved the old me but, more than anything, how I loved and protected the younger me.

It also taught me as a Black Fat Femme how powerful anger and spite can be. Much of who I used to be has shaped the person I am now and want to be as well as the person I want to leave behind for the world. That's why writing this book was so important to me; I wanted to make sure I had something I could leave behind for other Black Fat Femmes who, too, were on a journey to self-love and self-discovery, while offering them a moment to breathe while they process all the bullshit they've had to endure.

I know that (chocolate) chip on your shoulder because I used to have it too. The feeling of "why me?" in a world where it felt like others had it easier. The moments where people said my anger wouldn't serve me – I can now look back and say it actually has.

I needed that anger to keep pressing forward. I needed that anger so that I could stay alive.

While it's extremely unfair that Black Fat Femmes have to go through many of the things they have to go through to become who we are, we persist because we know we have to. That's the power of being a Black Fat Femme. No matter what folks have done to you, have done to us, we are still here thriving. We continue to lay a foundation for others who are watching us and learning from us. Those who often aren't seen or valued in traditional spaces, but know how bright their light shines.

I think what was so eye opening for me is recognizing that so much that the world puts on us as Black Fat Femmes isn't really about us. Projection is a b*tch, and she's often in every room we are in.

Folks want to know how or why we have a light. They want to know what freedom looks like and often can't fathom that it can be found through a 5'9", 300+ lb, cisgender male body in heels.

The world can't take it.

We continue to represent what triumph looks like – even when we often don't have anyone championing us. That is what makes our lives so beautiful. We really are roses in a world full of stones.

Yes, while we make it look easy, so much of who we are and who we've become isn't something that just manifests. This was something that I had to learn – that even with watching all the folks I have looked up to in my life, there was something in them that said, "I have to want to be here."

There has to be a desire to shine. There has to be a fire inside you that burns brighter than anything you've ever seen before. Being a Black Fat Femme means having to demand the life you want *and* need.

The truth of the matter is – rarely does anyone tell you this. Black Fat Femmes rarely have someone who sits down to tell you the process of how to take a life filled with lemons and how to make pie. No one gives you ingredients, and people sure as hell don't give you a cookbook with a recipe.

A lot of my doing as a Black Fat Femme has been built solely on vibes and prayer. I pray to the ancestors for guidance and for strength to get through my hardest moments.

That's exactly what I hope this book (and this chapter) is for you now – *a book of recipes to become the baddest b*tch known to the world.* If there is no other chapter you pay attention to, this is the one that's going to give you the tools you need to learn from my experiences and change the perspective that you not only have about your thinking, but the ways you move throughout life.

Now first, what I have learned in my own journey to bad b*tchery is that all of us are looking for validation in some form or fashion. We are all looking for someone to "clap us up." I know that I have a bad habit of this, and social media has only made it worse. I still sit thinking to myself, "Why am I not a bigger deal after all the things I've accomplished?" The truth is, it's because you're you. People don't expect a lot out of Black people. The world doesn't expect much out of queer people. They *for damn sure* don't expect a lot out of Black queer people. Thus, we aren't giving the same energy because rarely are folks affirmed to demand it or feel like they deserve it.

One of my goals with writing this book was to do exactly that – affirm the experiences you've had and let you know that regardless of where you are in life, you deserve to be celebrated. But sometimes you have to demand it, and having the words (or the energy) to do so can often feel overwhelming.

I have often fallen into the trap of waiting for people, specifically white cisgender people, to clap me up – when they don't even see us as whole people. I've learned as a Black Fat Femme that it's important for you to pop your sh*t – not just to egg yourself on, because you never know who else might need it too.

But there are rules and levels to this. You've gotta know that so much of you being who you are is staying one step ahead of the game, and that is what I am here to do. To put you on.

The first rule to being a bad b*tch is that you can't wait for the world to see your humanity. You have to demand it.

To be frank, throughout much of my life, I believed that if I could assimilate – meaning be less Black, less fat, or even less femme – the world would fall at my feet. What I didn't understand was that by doing so, I was doing exactly what the world wanted me to do.

Disappear.

It took many days (sometimes even years) for me to understand that, and there was a ton of heartache that I went through in the process, specifically in waiting for other cisgender men to find me attractive.

That is where the root of the harm begins. I was waiting for a community – specifically a white community – to see me and the beauty I brought to the world. However, racism, fatphobia, and homophobia would always find a way to disturb my peace, because you can't belong in a community that isn't committed to helping you belong. But, most importantly, you can't rest on others to make you feel valued.

As cheesy as it sounds, the work really has to start within you. I have always known it, but I hated knowing it. Now, I embrace it.

Next, you have to know that owning your bad b*tchery is knowing that you don't have to always make people happy or be loved in order to love yourself. As a recovering people pleaser, I learned that many of my identities were tied to people pleasing because . . . oppression.

When you're Black, you're trying to always get white people/ someone to like you. When you're fat, you want the world to see you beyond your body because the world often tells you that if you're not desirable, you're dispensable. When you're queer, you're always trying to find a place to belong – so you practically spend every waking hour of your day/life waiting for someone to cosign you.

But that is the object of oppression – to make sure those who hold privilege want to offer a little of it to you. I often ask people, "Do you want privilege or liberation?" and that's literally what being a bad b*tch is. It's knowing that you have the liberty to radically love every part of your intersectional identity.

Once I learned that, my whole world changed.

Lastly, becoming a bad b*tch is figuring out what brings you inner peace, and a lot of that is making peace with the things you can't change or don't want to change. Yeah, yeah, yeah – I know you probably want to throw this book out the window now – but that is truly the most important thing to learn.

Making peace with my past really helped me make peace with the life I am living now. I was desperate to be thin or to deny parts of my Black and queer identity. All of that was once part of my survival, but now that I know better, I do better, and that brings me so much peace.

When most people chat with me, they often quip, "You seem so at peace with yourself," and truly, I am. I recognize that so many of the things that happened to me were out of my control and I wasted so much energy and time trying to change them.

Part of owning your bad b*tch is owning *all* the bad that got you to your peaceful place. It's also recognizing that so much of what you've been through was never really about you.

The moment I made peace with the idea that a lot of the stories I shared had nothing to do with me and everything to do with how toxic the world is, then it became so much easier for me to push through a room like it was no one else's business, just like Miss J taught me.

Chapter 8

Redefining Authenticity

"You can't be what you can't see."

—Marian Wright Edelman

I've always been a people pleaser. Even when I don't think I am doing it, I'm doing it. So much of it began when I was a child, mainly because I was always worried about "someone finding me out" or not being pleased with how I show up in the world.

One of the things about being a people pleaser (and queer) for that matter is that you are always looking for acceptance. You are always hoping that everyone you meet likes you. You're also always worried about what someone might think about you; thus, you sometimes tone down a lot of who you are just to get that approval.

Sometimes I think it's the cult upbringing. Sometimes I wonder if it's because people around me also struggled with being people pleasers too. I saw it in so many friends and family members – people spending their whole lives waiting for the world to validate them, only for them to be sad and empty in the end.

Talk to anyone who was part of *any* devout religious organization and they will tell you that people pleasing becomes the core of who you are, and I still find myself fighting to not let the feeling of "please like me" or "please love me" be the core of who I am.

The thing I often tell people is that being a people pleaser – especially as a Black Fat Femme – can and will leave you feeling empty. You end up giving so much of yourself to so many people that you really have nothing left *for you*. That is why I find myself being drawn to the idea that part of being authentic means being real with yourself about what you want and what you need from others and how so much of that is rooted in protecting your magic. If you don't, you end up lost. You being lost not knowing who you are or *why* you are the way you are. You look in the mirror and have no idea who the person is staring back at you. For a long time, I truly had no idea who I was or who I wanted to be, and now I can tell myself that said journey was just a part of me finding my authentic self, and in all sincerity, it hasn't been easy.

The greatest struggle that I have had up to this point in my life is figuring out who I was outside of the trauma. You know – who I am when I take out my contact lenses and let my shoulders down. The person who doesn't feel like they always have to be mighty and strong in a world where Black Fat Femmes have to save everyone, including themselves.

The heart of the matter is that so much of me not being able to know who I am or who I want to be is because I never had time to think about it. That's the thing no one ever seems to want to talk about (or gives us space to process) – the ways in which so many Black Fat Femmes are just trying to survive that they barely have time to think about who they are or about the person they want to be.

I can think of moments in my life, especially when I first got my first "adult" job, where I watched others be their "authentic" selves and wished I could be like them. But there was always something in my mind that said, "What will others think?" or "Will this cost me an opportunity now or later?"

Moreover, I also just didn't have the time. I never had a moment to think about "Who am I?" outside of everything that everyone in the world kept trying to put on me. Religion. Hypermasculinity. Anti-Blackness. Misogynoir. Oppression.

When you are marginalized, this becomes so much of your story – you never really get to know who *you* are because you spend so much time trying to jump over the hurdles that life has set out for you.

This, more than anything, is what often leads us to live in the cycle of depression and anxiety. It was something that I was trying to fight for so long because I was trying to be "strong," not realizing how much harm I was doing to myself.

This led me to resort back to the little me, standing on those stairs scared that I was going to get spanked for being too girly. The little boy who was once told that the world hated the sound of my voice. The little boy who was bullied for being too sure of myself.

Fear became who I was as a person.

Being "myself" made me believe that I could lose approval from friends. It made me worried about what my family might think of me (even though so many of them weren't even in my life in my later years) or even what my partner would think.

I can recall buying some heels and hiding them in my apartment because I didn't want my now husband to know I had them. Even when I thought I was being my most authentic self, there were still parts of me that I hid. There were parts of me that I was afraid to share with the world.

Now reflecting on it (and giving myself the space and time to process it), I can also understand *why* I was so afraid to be my authentic self. Why even with me seeing myself as a bad b*tch, I was still worried about how said bad b*tchiness would be received.

"You're too emotional," one person once told me. They even went on to say that me wearing my heart out on my sleeve would keep me from excelling in life. However, now I understand that the parts of me that were "emotional" were the parts of me that were crying out to be seen and validated. Parts of me were hiding in the shadows. The authentic me wanted the world to know that being me wasn't the problem.

It was the world that had a problem.

I quickly realized that regardless of how queer/femme I was in this life, people were going to have an issue with it. That is why now I preach a ministry of me not being everyone's cup of tea. I also tell people to grab some water if they don't like how authentic I am because they probably need it anyway.

Now, I have no choice but to be authentic. I have no choice but to wake up and think to myself, "You have to be you and love every part of that – because that is the only thing going to keep you alive."

I now preach a ministry of authenticity because there is no other way for Black Fat Femmes to survive. But it's not to say that being your authentic self doesn't come without its challenges.

It's about redefining the idea of authenticity so you can in fact live your best life.

There's this vast misconception that every Black Fat Femme just wakes up one day and says, "I'm *Gone with the Wind* fabulous." As you can *clearly* see, it took me almost 8 chapters and 30-something years to get to a place where I could wake up and say that I liked the person I saw in the mirror. And if it were that easy, I'd probably have more books published about it.

But the reality is that even with understanding the definition of "authenticity," I had to redefine it for myself, because even that gave me cause for pause.

For years, I struggled with the term, because when people often use the word, it's coded with undertones that read, "I like you, but I don't like your *lifestyle*." You know, it's almost like a backhanded compliment. It feels like a microaggression because rarely can someone say, "I like you because I think that you exist in a world working overtime to eradicate you."

That's what I would love to hear, but here we are.

Whenever someone uses the word to describe me, I almost freeze. It's like a white person going to touch my hair or being called "well spoken." It just feels gross. "Resilient" is also another word I hate for folks to use to describe me, but I also (now) recognize that a lot of that is me projecting from my own lived experiences and feeling like that is all I have ever had to be. Resilient.

I never understood why so many people would resort to using *that* word to describe me when all I've ever really wanted to do was live and be loved. But if there is anything that living this long has taught me, authenticity is something that many people fear, which is why it's such a shock when Black Fat Femmes show up in the world unfazed by the oppression and scrutiny they face.

But it also tells me, when someone uses the word, that they know and understand what I am up against as a Black Fat Femme. It also tells me that they know their privilege and what they could do to make it easier for people like me.

But even with the way the word *authenticity* makes me feel, I have learned the importance of embracing it. I have also

Redefining Authenticity

learned how important it is for me to tell other queer folks to embrace that word too.

■ ■ ■

Something someone I loved once told me is that you can't comprehend your future if you don't take a look at the past. While so much of this book has been rooted in my lived experience, I never realized how so much of my struggle in wanting to be my authentic self was rooted in what I now know as a culture of fear.

However, before I continue, I think it's important to engage the definition of what it means to be authentic since so much of this chapter is about exactly that (and why so many people in the world seem to have a problem with Black Fat Femmes being authentic).

Authenticity, put simply, is the idea of being one's true self. It includes one's own personality, value, and spirit, regardless of the pressure you're under to act otherwise. So much of this book details the various pressures I along with other Black Fat Femmes in media have had to endure, but I have yet to fully engage *why* the world takes issue with Black Fat Femmes – or anyone for that matter – being their authentic selves.

The only explanation I've ever had around why so many people have issues with me or people like me is fear.

Fear runs the world. "If you don't like it, fear it. Do everything in your power to get rid of it, because even though I don't fully understand it, it's dangerous." Fear is used as a tool to keep the world from being who they truly want to be.

Fear is what kept me from liking me. Fear kept me from loving me. But it took me years to fully understand the definition of both authenticity and fear and see how the two words go hand and hand.

It's always been and will always be about control. If someone can keep you from being authentic and celebrating the parts of who you are, then it makes it so much easier to keep you in fear. You begin to want to hide or even more, not want to live. But it's nothing new. The world has always tried to keep Black Fat Femmes living in fear.

A quick history lesson: from the 1966 Compton Cafeteria Riots in San Francisco, California, where Black drag queens and trans people were violently harassed to the 1969 Stonewall Riots in New York City where Marsha P. Johnson had to incite a riot to find her peace, control has always been the goal. Systems of oppression have always wanted Black people, queer people, and Black queer people to live in fear.

I even think a lot about what happened to Bayard Rustin in his time of working with Dr. Martin Luther King. Thinking about the ways that both community members and the law worked to try to silence Bayard by arresting him for being his authentic self in a time where queer people were supposed to not exist.

But the beauty in all of this is that so much of what has happened in the past is leading the charge on what we are seeing now as Black Fat Femme representation and what it means to authentically share your story, and that is why it's so important for you not to dim your light.

I think a lot about the dolls of *RuPaul's Drag Race* often and how poorly they are treated after leaving the show. I have seen the terrible things bloggers post about LaLa Ri or Bob the Drag Queen. I have seen the ways in which the RuPaul fandom has gone after Black queens for demanding that white fans treat them with more love and respect.

Let's not even get into the debacle of what happened to Mayhem Miller in 2022 that caused her to have to lock up all of her social media accounts because someone wouldn't stop sending her hate messages. More than anything, I think a lot about Silky Nutmeg Ganache from season 11 of *Drag Race* and how unfair and cruel the world was to her during her time on the show.

Silky, a standout contestant in her season who showcased her charisma, uniqueness, nerve, and talent, captivated audiences not only with her larger-than-life personality but also with her unapologetic stance on her lived experience, making many of the other contestants uncomfortable on the show. Throughout the season, Silky courageously confronted the intersectional challenges she faced as a Black, plus-sized queen navigating the competitive world of drag.

She remained vocal about her lived experience and how often so many people doubted her because of her size, race, and the way she performed gender. In a realm where glamour and polish are often the only thing that makes you "worthy," Silky fearlessly challenged stereotypes and pushed back against societal norms that often marginalized individuals like her. Her journey on the show was a testament to resilience and self-confidence in the face of adversity. Despite being doubted and underestimated by some, Silky constantly proved that drag is not only about appearance but also about the strength of character and individuality.

But instead of the world embracing the likes of Silky and Mayhem Miller, they used fear to try to shrink them and their light. Something that happens to Black Fat Femmes over and over again.

The reality is that the world has and will continue to doubt us, because the world will never be able to understand what we've been through to get this far in life. When I look at Silky, even though I may not know her personally, I know her story. I know the moments in life that someone looked at her and dismissed her as just another "loud, Black, fat queen."

But it doesn't just impact drag queens. I recall talking to Dexter Mayfield about the profound impact he has had on the dance world, despite the challenges and prejudices he has faced both in front of and behind the industry. How much his journey is a testament to resilience being that we both work in an industry that judges you before it truly knows or understands how hard your walk can be.

In the dance world, where physical appearance can dictate opportunities, Dexter has courageously defied stereotypes and shattered barriers by simply being in spaces where he knows his is not wanted. His presence challenges the notion that dancers must fit a specific mold, showcasing that talent and passion transcend size or societal expectations.

Dexter's personal experiences of being labeled the "fat friend" highlight the pervasive fatphobia and body shaming that exist not only in dance but throughout society. Despite these challenges, Dexter has embraced his body and his talent, refusing to diminish his personality to make others more comfortable. His confidence and charisma command attention, proving that true artistry knows no bounds.

Conversations with Dexter reveal the emotional toll of navigating an industry that often overlooks or marginalizes those who don't fit traditional standards of beauty. His resilience in the face of adversity inspires others to embrace their authentic selves fully, regardless of external judgment.

Beyond his dance prowess, Dexter has become a beacon of body positivity and self-acceptance. Through his advocacy and visibility, he has sparked important dialogues about inclusivity

Redefining Authenticity

and representation in dance and beyond. His journey reminds us that diversity in all its forms enriches our communities and challenges us to rethink what it means to be talented and successful.

Watching both of these people move in the industry, it reminded me of what so many Black Fat Femmes have shared with me. It's not about us not being able to be authentic, it's about how afraid the world is of us being authentic. And we internalize that.

It's the judgment we face. It's knowing that even in moments where we are not worried about our race, size, or presentation, the world is fixated on it. We are often made to feel uncomfortable about who we are because the world is uncomfortable with who *they* are.

It's understanding that we have always lived in a world where those in positions of power are doing everything in their power to discourage anyone and everyone from being their authentic selves, because they understand the power in that.

But it's more than that, it's also about our livelihood. It's the world knowing how much power someone relinquishes when they allow queer people, specifically Black Fat Femmes, the ability to thrive. "Being who you want to be without needing my validation" is probably the most powerful thing that anyone could do.

So much of authenticity is about audacity; Black Fat Femmes having the audacity to say that they not only won't be silent about who they are, but that they like who they are.

The audacity of embracing one's authentic self as a Black Fat Femme in a world that often seeks to silence or marginalize such identities is profound. It's about boldly affirming one's worth and beauty in a society that too often measures value based on narrow, exclusionary standards. This audacity challenges the status quo and demands recognition of the richness and diversity of human experience.

Audacity in self-acceptance is not just a personal triumph; it is a revolutionary act that inspires others to embrace their own truths and challenge oppressive systems. It encourages solidarity and empowerment within marginalized communities, fostering a collective resilience against prejudice and bigotry.

It's about reclaiming power and agency over one's narrative. It is about refusing to conform to external pressures and instead embracing authenticity with unwavering confidence. Because how dare I, someone who has every identity that the world hates, like who I am?

It's really about you liking you. It's about giving yourself the gumption to look in the mirror and say, "Wow, I really am a work of art."

This was something for years I was too afraid to say. I was too afraid to look in the mirror and give myself credit for the person I have become because not only was I worried about what other people thought about that person, I was so worried about being someone else.

But please don't blame yourself. The world celebrates this. White supremacy celebrates this.

However, it wasn't until I understood this: knowing the world hates me and still having the audacity to show up as my authentic self (and *loving* my authentic self) is how we undo these oppressive systems.

For so much of my life, it was about trying to control my appearance to the world, because I feared that being different would bring me unwanted negative attention. But the truth of the matter is that the world has already covertly told me what it thinks about me, so now I move with the energy of "Who gives a fu*k?"

Redefining Authenticity

I know the world rarely wants to celebrate anyone who is fearlessly navigating spaces publicly and saying "No matter what you try to do, I am still going to love myself more than you could ever comprehend." Rarely will the world give me my credit for overcoming all the obstacles I faced, obstacles that have made me proud enough to finally sit down and put them in this book.

It has been and will always be about me loving myself more than what the world wants to give me credit for. It's also about me preaching a gospel that encourages other Black Fat Femmes to love who they are, too.

The thing is, I know what it's like to look in the mirror and see a reflection and think, "How can I love myself when no one else does?" You have probably been through things that I might never be able to fully comprehend, or you might even think that I am preaching from a place of privilege because I now have a (self-made) platform that is garnering popular attention for the things I say and do.

Regardless of how you feel about me (or even yourself for that matter), the ministry of authenticity I preach is one that tells you that whatever unhealthy expectations you have of yourself in this life, know that you can let those go. Whatever fear you have about embracing the person you want to be and the fear you have about how that might hinder you in life – let that go too.

None of it has ever served us. It also won't save you either.

To know that you deserve the right to live authentically means you now have the power to control not only yourself but also how others treat you. This was something that I always struggled with in life – partly because I felt like I deserved a lot of the mistreatment I got.

But, embracing my authentic self helped me to understand that liking me *and* loving me also means standing up for me. It meant me having to teach others how to treat me and how to talk about me and people like me.

I think the hardest part of my journey in coming into my authentic self was just that: not letting people talk to me or treat me in any kind of way. As a child, specifically as a Black child, you sometimes just learn to accept that "that's how people are." They are going to say mean-spirited things to you or about you, and you just kind of let it slide. But something I quickly learned (thanks in part to therapy) is how so much of that damages the parts of you that you might like.

For me, it was my femininity. It was the moments that I felt soft and emotionally connected to myself. It was the moments where so much of my softness was connected to the feelings of my mother and other women, specifically trans women, that made me feel loved and beautiful.

When I began to unpack so much of why I let people be mean to me, disrespect me, or dunk on my authenticity, I quickly realized how much of it was because that is what I thought I deserved. It was me not knowing that I was worth more that I was giving myself credit for. It was me not understanding that telling other people how to respect me was me letting go of all the terrible things in my life that I felt I deserved as a Black Fat Femme.

Therapy became my sanctuary, a space where I could unravel the tangled threads of self-doubt and reclaim my inherent worth. It wasn't just about learning coping mechanisms or gaining insight; it was a transformative journey of self-discovery and self-empowerment. In those sessions, I confronted the narratives I had internalized about my identity – narratives shaped by societal prejudice and personal experiences of marginalization.

One of the most profound revelations was recognizing how societal attitudes toward Blackness, femininity, and queerness intersected to diminish my sense of self-worth. From a young age, I had absorbed harmful stereotypes and discriminatory behaviors directed toward me. Whether it was casual insults or systemic biases, these experiences chipped away at my confidence and reinforced a distorted self-image.

Moreover, as a Black Fat Femme, navigating these intersections meant contending with layers of prejudice and discrimination that often went unacknowledged or were minimized in mainstream narratives. The societal expectation to conform to Eurocentric beauty standards, heteronormative ideals, and gender binaries further complicated my journey toward self-acceptance. It required dismantling not only external judgments but also internalized shame and self-criticism.

Through therapy, I learned the importance of setting boundaries and advocating for myself. I discovered that asserting my worth was not synonymous with arrogance but rather an act of self-preservation. It meant reclaiming my right to define how others treat me and rejecting the notion that mistreatment was somehow justified by my identity.

In embracing my authentic self, I found strength in vulnerability and resilience in self-compassion. It was about honoring the parts of myself that had been silenced or dismissed, celebrating my multifaceted identity, and embracing the intersections that make me uniquely who I am. It was a journey toward self-love that required courage, patience, and a willingness to challenge societal norms that sought to diminish my worth.

Today, I continue to navigate the complexities of identity with a renewed sense of purpose and clarity. I recognize that my journey is ongoing and that healing is not linear. There are moments of triumph and setbacks, but each experience contributes to my growth and understanding of myself.

My journey toward embracing my authentic self as a Black Fat Femme has been transformative. It has been about reclaiming my narrative, challenging societal expectations, and honoring the resilience of my identity. Through therapy and self-reflection, I have learned that I am worthy of love, respect, and dignity – and that my voice deserves to be heard, loud and clear.

It was fully understanding that me being authentic not just with myself but in this world meant that I was disrupting established norms and expectations while challenging others to confront their biases and preconceptions.

I was taking back so much of my personal power – something I felt like I never fully had.

For those that know me, they know I spend a lot of time talking about personal power and how it connects to authenticity because I don't believe we talk about it enough. I don't think Black Fat Femmes ever get the space to think about what it means for them to be powerful in a world that is hell-bent in taking our voice, power, and lives away.

But so much of this book is just that: me putting down in words how to find your personal power. You need to tell the world, "You can't break what you didn't make." So much of the authentic me you see is grit. It's the moments I have had to be the person *I* wanted to be, not what the world wanted me to be.

That's what matters most. It's who *you* want to be.

■ ■ ■

While I've spent most of this chapter talking about being authentic, I have to acknowledge the risks that come with living in a ministry of authenticity. I have seen others deal with it. Hell, I even lived it for a short time in my life.

When you are authentic, you are going to make people uncomfortable. For some, me being my authentic self unearths feelings in others that they are often too afraid to deal with.

I can picture candidly the times in my life, specifically in my older years, where someone would look at me in my heels or at my nails and try to compute how I could be so happy knowing that the world is gawking at me in disapproval.

I even watched an entire family stop what they were doing to stare at me as I was leaving an airport carousel, them trying to figure out my gender and why I as a "man" would want to be in heels and makeup.

While others might think of these moments and cringe, I thought about them as my superpower. I now think a lot about how being a Black Fat Femme is my superpower, considering that I have the power to live in the heads of others, freely.

But more than anything, the struggle that the world has with my superpower and my authenticity is that of projection. So many people can't conceive the idea of being free. To me, being a Black Fat Femme is that. Freedom. I am free from societal expectations that I never agreed to live up to in the first place.

People are fearful of authenticity because authenticity demands honesty and vulnerability, qualities that can be unsettling in a world accustomed to facades and conformity. It reminds people that they too can live without limitations, and for some people, specifically by cisgender heteronormative standards, that is scary.

It's scary to think "I don't care what you think about me" because your whole life you are taught to care. You are taught

174

to care what your family thinks, what your friends think, and even what God and the angels above you think.

Yet, it is precisely through embracing authenticity that true connections are forged, boundaries are respected, and genuine understanding can thrive. It is a courageous path that invites others to see and accept the richness of diversity in all its forms.

When you exist at the intersection of being Black and queer, the world can feel like a stage where every move is scrutinized. It's as though you carry within you the weight of histories – the struggle against systemic oppression, the fight for civil rights, and the ongoing battle for LGBTQ+ equality.

Navigating this intersectionality requires a delicate balance of asserting your identity while confronting the prejudices and stereotypes that seek to diminish your presence. As a Black queer individual, visibility becomes your armor as it encourages others to do the same. It tells others that there is strength in numbers, and while the world may not want to see you or your vitality, you being in the world is unduly powerful.

More than that, it's necessary to break down the systems that were created to demean us. It's a reminder that the scrutiny you face isn't just about personal choices; it reflects broader societal attitudes and ingrained biases that perpetuate discrimination. It underscores the importance of representation and the power of storytelling in reshaping narratives and fostering empathy and understanding.

In this complex landscape, you walk the line of visibility being both your shield and ammo.

For us, the act of simply existing is compelling. Each day becomes a negotiation between asserting one's identity and navigating a world that often refuses to acknowledge the legitimacy of your identity. It is a delicate dance where one must balance self-expression with self-preservation, authenticity with caution.

I am by no means telling you to put yourself in direct harm, but I am telling you that with great risk comes great reward. Every day that I wake up and walk out the door, I am making the ancestors proud. That is the thing I spend the most time thinking about. How can I make those who came before me proud?

It's also knowing that none of what we experience is new. In the face of pervasive discrimination, embracing one's true self becomes an act of defiance against the forces that seek to diminish or erase individuality. It is a refusal to conform to narrow expectations and a demand to be seen and valued on one's own terms. This journey toward self-acceptance is not without its challenges. It requires courage to confront the internalized prejudices and societal barriers that can hinder personal growth and fulfillment. Much of what the world does is a response to your greatness.

Yet, within this struggle lies a profound opportunity for growth and connection. By embracing their authentic selves, individuals create spaces where others can also feel safe to do the same. It fosters communities built on mutual respect and understanding, where diversity is not only tolerated but celebrated. These spaces become sanctuaries from the relentless gaze of judgment and bigotry, offering solace and support to those who have long been marginalized.

In the quest for equality, visibility plays a crucial role. It is through visibility that stereotypes are shattered and myths debunked. When individuals boldly proclaim their identities, they challenge preconceived notions and broaden society's understanding of what it means to be Black and queer. They become beacons of hope for others who may be struggling to reconcile their own identities with societal expectations.

Moreover, authenticity cultivates resilience. It empowers individuals to navigate adversity with strength and grace, knowing that their worth is inherent and not contingent upon the acceptance of others. This self-assurance is an important tool in the fight against discrimination and injustice, fueling movements for social change and inspiring others to stand up for their rights.

It is important to acknowledge that the journey toward authenticity is not a solitary one. Know that there are folks like myself working day in and day out to remind the world that we not just exist but that we *deserve* to persist.

I want you to think of this chapter as the first step to understanding that so much of the emotions and pain that you have experienced are valid, but they shouldn't define the foundation of who you are. Happiness is indeed relative, and I acknowledge that some may perceive my perspective as coming from a place of privilege. However, it's crucial to recognize that this sense of contentment and self-assurance is something I've worked hard to cultivate, and that is what I want for you, too.

Acknowledging the validity of your emotions and experiences is not about dwelling in pain or allowing it to dictate your identity. It's about honoring your journey, recognizing the challenges you've overcome, and embracing the growth that comes from adversity.

Finding happiness and fulfillment despite societal expectations or personal hardships is a journey toward self-empowerment and resilience, and while it might not happen tomorrow, knowing that it's possible is what gives me hope. It's what keeps my glass half full in a world that is constantly trying to knock the glass out of my hand.

The journey to self-discovery and acceptance is about recognizing the inherent worthiness of your own happiness and authenticity. It's about recognizing that being authentically happy means not letting others live in your head rent free. Navigating toward self-love involves understanding that your identity transcends the judgments and constraints imposed by others, many of which stem from societal limitations.

It's knowing and fully accepting that we as Black Fat Femmes have every right to be happy, not just in our bodies, but in our lives too. As I move forward, I want to challenge you to not just like yourself, but to love yourself fearlessly. That is the only way I know how to move, and I hope by the end of this book, you can move that way too.

Chapter 9

Remaining Black, Fat, and Visibly Queer

Vis·i·ble: Able to be seen.

I often get asked where my passion for media representation began. A lot of it started with being a latchkey kid who honestly spent way too much time in front of the television while my (single) mother was at work.

But it wasn't just because the media was fun. I always felt like the media, specifically television and film, was hinting at a life that I could have in a time where I hated so much about my own. In a lot of ways, television and media were always my great escape, connecting me to people I wished I could be like or people I wished I knew.

In my head, all the folks I mentioned in my story up to this point were my sisters. They were my mentors. They were my chosen family that didn't judge me for being who I was or for who I was longing to be. They were folks who understood everything I had been through, and even if they never knew I existed, it was enough for me to exist knowing that they did.

Media, in a strange way, validated me even before "Doctor-JonPaul" became a thing. I can remember being on Myspace and Facebook in my earlier years and posting about the things I dreamed of wanting to do, things I wished I would have done or even about the ways that certain television shows were helping me to *find* me.

The validation I got – both online and off – let me know not just how powerful my voice was but how powerful the media was in shaping it. It also helped validate many of the areas of me that I needed to heal, especially when I would find a sad character from a television show to latch on to and wallow in my own moments of misery. I'm thankful for the friends both then and now who helped me snap out of it.

But even then, I didn't have the full lexicon to explain why I was so bothered by white queer shows and knew there was something off about the media. I knew that *my* story was missing – not just in real life but also on shows that I watched.

I think about how many times I saw shows like *Jerry Springer* and *Jenny Jones* villainize queer people for "hiding their secrets." I also remember vividly the shows on *Maury* where they would spend hours, almost days, on "is she a man or a woman?" and seeing people get so angry when they thought they were being "tricked" into believing that a trans woman was passable.

Honestly, the early days of media made life so scary for me, and I can only imagine how much worse it has gotten for folks on social media. I don't take the platform I have now lightly, which is why I have committed so much of my work to debunking the miseducation that media and media pundits put out into the world.

When you're watching a television show and everyone in the crowd is booing you and throwing things at you simply for existing, it makes the world a very, very scary place.

But I never really understood how powerful media was until I got to college and opted to study it. In the first few years of my college experience at California State University,

San Bernardino, I was committed to making content for television and film, but I often got shut down by white instructors who often told me that my stories were "too complex" or that there wasn't a market for them.

Add to the equation that I was bad at math and couldn't pass Accounting 1 or Statistics and had a 1.9 grade point average. One day my lifesaver and forever mentor Carolyn pulled me to the side in her office. "Mr. Higgins!" I could hear her yelling down the hall. "Come in here for a sec."

After scolding me in her office about being on academic probation and reminding me why I was in college, she told me to change my major to communications. "We need more people like you in the field," she led with. "You like to critique systems. You have a very critical eye for the media. I can just tell."

She was right. I had spent months, if not years, in high school building a website where I would talk about all the films and television shows that inspired me. While at this time there were only a few Black characters I could identify with, I knew she was on to something after I had spent almost one full hour going over my hot take on why the 1985 film *The Color Purple* was one of the best films ever made.

After changing my major to communications, I remember taking as many classes as I could that would offer me a chance to critique avenues of media. The struggles I began to have in the program (not because the content was hard) began when I started pushing back on all the ways the white men in media courses were taking up space.

"Where are our stories?" I once asked a professor.
"What do you mean?" he rebutted.

Remaining Black, Fat, and Visibly Queer

"Black stories. Queer stories? Stories about Black queer people who actually have something to say?"

I can tell he didn't know how to answer. In fairness, I don't think he could, because at that time in the media, there were only a handful of Black queer people who were speaking about their experiences publicly.

"Well, you got RuPaul!" he joked. This is why if you know me, it's one of the reasons I jokingly say that all roads lead to RuPaul Charles (and that is why I mention him often in a lot of my work).

After spending years in these classrooms with white men telling me that the best "queer" representations were films and television shows written by white cisgender straight men, I told myself that I wouldn't let up on trying to find them. I would spend as much of my life as necessary challenging entertainment spaces to see me through the lenses of my intersectional identity, even if it meant me being frustrated in the process.

As I continued in the program, I became known as the "social justice" student. I was the student most professors feared having in their class because they knew I was going to challenge elements of what we learned for being rooted in whiteness. Also, going to a predominantly white institution and being the vice president of the Black Student Alliance and the president of the Gay Straight Alliance didn't help.

It was in my junior year that I took a "Gender, Race & Media" course where the white male professor told me something that another colleague would tell me later in some years: "If you want accurate representation, you have to be committed to making it happen."

At that time, being a young, bright-eyed, and bushy-tailed 20-something, I went off into the world saying, "That's exactly what I'll do. I'll break my back to create it. I will work overtime to make sure that I see myself in all forms of media."

Now, as a 30-something adult who has worked in rooms with some of the top producers, writers, and executives, I've learned that advice was my introduction into being gaslit. It was a quick way for my white educator to not have to take accountability for the ways he and many of his counterparts ice out Black queer representation in the media.

It was those classes that told me media would forever be this way if I didn't call it out. It was those classes that reminded me why it was so important for me to keep being vocal about representation – even after years of being told (and shown) that my story as a Black queer person didn't matter.

After spending multiple weeks in Art of Film classes and other classes that fed me the belief that the only "great" stories were the ones that uplifted the (white) queer narrative, I made sure I called it out. Every film. Every show. Every opportunity.

I wanted the world to know that Black queer stories were important and that I didn't care where I was in the world; I was going to make the world care.

Later in life when I graduated and began teaching women's studies, I quickly learned how the rhetoric that our stories weren't as important as "others" persisted when my students began to challenge the source materials of my courses.

"Why do we need to watch *Paris Is Burning*? Why do we need to watch *Pose*?" my students would ask.

In part, I chose these materials because now I was the one who was in control of my classroom, but also because I was tired of being asked to teach queer, white-centered material. I wanted students to know and understand something greater than a film like *This Boy's Life* that centered only on the main character's sexuality. I wanted folks to see true representation – moments where people, not just characters, were able to be visibly queer.

■ ■ ■

I spend so much time talking about the need to amplify our voices because media was the only thing I had that I felt validated me growing up. Watching television was truly a safety blanket for me, especially being someone who always dreamed of being in the limelight.

When I got old enough to understand what it was I was dealing with in terms of my own identity, I quickly learned how much media played into that and decided that it would be up to me to use whatever platform I had to change it. Media shapes people's lives. It shapes people's narratives, but more than anything, it often helps people figure out who they are in a world where they are being told who they have to be.

But it's the moments of my life where I was being gaslit into believing that I was the one oppressing myself that helped me realize how important media was in my life. I think back to my younger "blogger" years and how grateful I was to see someone like a B. Scott online in the late 2000s talking openly about transphobia and anti-Blackness. It was important for me to see them on YouTube naming many of the things I was dealing with in my own dorm room, especially at a time where media spaces weren't highlighting Black femme voices. And let's not even get into talking about the ways media spaces villainized fat people. I probably could write another book on that alone.

Though, so much of my advocacy and love for advocating for Black Fat Femme voices in the media isn't just about me wanting a platform. It comes from a place of knowing what it's like *not* to have the representation you need at the most pivotal time in your life when you really need it.

I know what it's like to look around and see so many other identities being celebrated and feel alone in my intersectional experience. I needed more Black Fat Femme characters in my children's books. I needed more Black Fat Femme characters in my cartoons. I needed them in my television shows and in my movies just so that I could know that me and my existence mattered.

I often think about how so many people assume that just because I grew up in Southern California – a place that's deemed liberal/accepting by most standards – that it automatically translates to "being seen" and not needing that visibility. I would honestly love to spend more time talking about the ways society celebrates California as a queer mecca when in truth it's just as racist, homophobic, and transphobic as any other state – but that's a different chapter in a different book.

For anyone who lives near Los Angeles, California (or Hollywood), you know that there is a certain look, skin color, and type of "person" who is often held in high regard. This often translates to a certain "look" that is seen in media, specifically a certain type of influencer, writer, or media personality. Meaning: white, cisgender presenting, and slim. This is why for years I thought I was going to be the Black Will Truman from *Will & Grace* and have a life where everyone would throw glitter anytime I walked into the room.

I talk openly about media representation because even now, with all that I have accomplished (and will accomplish), I know that the standard in media will always be white, cis, heterosexual, and male. In all, the point that I am trying to make is that young Black queer babies need to see more Black queer people in all facets of their life. They also need to see them alive and well.

What's even more disconcerting is how I grew up in a place that is sold as being one of the most liberal places to live but have always felt unseen. Even at my now big age, I *still* feel unseen. While I am grateful for some of the strides Hollywood and the media have tried to make in the last few years with inclusion – specifically with getting a whole season centered on a Black Fat Femme character in Laurie Nunn's *Sex Education* – it's still not enough.

But that is the gist of what this book is about: the ways that society tells Black Fat Femmes that their representation, even if it's bad or not fully accurate, is good representation. But none of that representation matters when you have no idea how to make sense of your journey or when you do not have a single thing on television that gives you a glimmer of hope that life could be better. I think much of my devotion to speaking out about queer representation in the media comes from a place of understanding the impact that representation has on television.

Representation sparks creativity. Representation creates possibilities, possibilities that so many Black Fat Femmes are told – both overtly and covertly – are never possible.

Representation for me told me that I could start a podcast. It told me I could get this book sold, and it told me I could create a brand that tells people they have the right to authentically celebrate themselves.

Why I believe it's so important to keep talking about Black Fat Femme representation is knowing how close I live to the places that create these stories and yet how alone I felt. I can't imagine what someone living in middle America feels like. I can't imagine what a little Black Fat Femme kid in the depths of the South feels like, knowing that they might never see or know someone who celebrates them.

Even though we now have social media and there seems to be a growing number of influencers and media figures who are trying to challenge media to be more inclusive, it's simply not enough when so many of the stories we hear and see about youth unaliving themselves involve Black Fat Femme kids. While these stories often aren't publicized, working with LGBTQ+ youth I know this to be true, and that is why I was so intent on writing this book.

Our stories aren't just needed for us to survive. Our stories are needed in order for us to *thrive*.

Every day I think to myself how much different my life would have been had I been able to see more Black, Fat, and Femme people in my life, both in real life and on television. And not just existing either. Living full, whole lives. I often think, "What if I had *Noah's Arc* in my teens, and I didn't have to wait 'til college to experience it? What different decisions would I have made? Who would I have become?"

I think about all of the money I probably would have saved in therapy. I probably wouldn't have let so many people (and men) take advantage of me because I would have valued myself just a little bit more.

Even with all that I have accomplished up to this point in my life, the lack of representation in the media sometimes keeps me feeling small and wondering if I will ever fully love the person I have come to be. While it's getting easier to do, the truth is that it is lonely to feel like you are always the only one being the person to do what you are doing.

I have to be my own cheerleader because the industry and the world refuses to give me my shine.

In addition, people aren't talking about the struggles Black Fat Femmes have in making their dreams come true, or what

Remaining Black, Fat, and Visibly Queer

struggles we navigate in building our own tables when we often don't even have the right tools or directions to build.

I can recall growing up and watching Disney cartoons and shows thinking to myself, "Will I ever have a happy ending?" It was the constant feeling of turning on the television and feeling that both love and success were fleeting. And I felt that if I did stand up and celebrate myself, something bad was going to happen to me.

Let's not forget that the Black and queer representation that *does exist* is mostly rooted in talks of our demise, specifically when talking about AIDS and the HIV epidemic. In other words, Black queer media representation has always been rooted in stories of pain, specifically driving the stigma that all Black queer people have HIV or AIDS.

If it wasn't HIV or AIDS, it was Black queer people being ousted by their families *while* having HIV and AIDS and dying alone. This idea was pounded into my head as a child, making me believe that there wasn't any other way for my story to end.

This says a lot about what folks in our world think about Black queer people and their narratives. People are disconnected from us and what light we shine in the world.

But it's not just about our stories, it's also about how seeing someone in the media like you can make you feel not alone. Having versed stories helps speak to the multitudes we as Black Fat Femmes have, and media can play a big role in us finding ourselves, especially when you live in the headspace that there is no one else like you in the world.

If anything, this chapter is a reflection on how powerful media is and how necessary it is for young Black Fat Femmes who need to hear and see stories that validate them. While there were a handful of people who helped shape my life that I mention in previous chapters, the media did a piss-poor job of giving me insight into who they were outside of their personas. And it is still that way.

I didn't have access to their stories. I couldn't sit down with them and learn the ins and outs of what they had been through to get to where they were in life. I couldn't talk with them about all the ways the media told me to hate myself and how not seeing other happy Black Fat Femmes almost sent me to meet my maker.

Growing up, I didn't know them. I didn't have direct access to them to say, "Hey, I need someone like you in my life so I can keep living." It wasn't until I was able to garner a social media following that I felt like the things I had to say about representation and media mattered. But my social media following has taught me that my voice, my work, and this book are essential, because there are many people who too feel the same way I do.

More than anything, the worst part of today's state of media is how passively flippant some folks are about my needing to be more inclusive of our voices and stories.

Once, in sharing my frustration, I mentioned only seeing "positive" white queer stories being uplifted in the media to someone, and they responded, "But what about RuPaul?" RuPaul is and has always been the go-to answer for anyone who is asked about Black queer representation in the media, mainly because he's the only Black queer person that white people know.

As if I could *really* sit down with RuPaul, a man who has been slender his whole life, and talk about all the things I have been through as a Black, fat, queer girl in my life. A poor one at that.

As if one Black queer celebrity is going to represent everything that all Black Fat Femme people experience.

Even reflecting on the early years of VH1's *The RuPaul Show* (I told you that all roads lead us to RuPaul and *RuPaul's Drag Race*), there were so many problematic plot points with that show, specifically the lack of conversation about gender and identity and the ways people sold RuPaul as a caricature. Even now, with *RuPaul's Drag Race* being the force that it is, there still continues to be conversations about the ways in which Black Fat Femmes are often exploited and emotionally harmed on the show and the ways that RuPaul never steps up to protect us, even with all the power and access he might have.

And yes, I have openly written about that too (and gotten a lot of pushback from folks in media).

"But that's how it has been and how it will always be."

Well, that's what they want you to believe as a Black Fat Femme. The powers that be want you to believe that you should be okay with just a glimmer of hope. They think you should settle for the small glimpse of "hope" that one film or television gives you every 5–10 years.

I sometimes think about what the younger me could have learned if they saw someone like playwright Michael R. Jackson writing and winning awards for their work. Maybe I wouldn't have given up on my dream of writing a book when I was younger because I believed that no one wanted to read a book about the Black Fat Femme experience.

Maybe I wouldn't have given up on my dreams of actually working in entertainment in college and would have told myself to keep pushing forward because my voice, my thoughts, and my experiences were both valid and needed in the media.

Or maybe I would have felt that much less alone knowing that there were other creators like Rob Milton who were using music and storytelling to help them heal from years of pain. Or even a Preston Mitchum, speaker and civil rights advocate, who isn't afraid to say what needs to be said and hold people accountable for the things they do to harm Black Fat Femmes in the media.

For Black Fat Femmes, visibility isn't just about being seen – it's about validation of our existence in a world that is driven by and shaped by media perception.

But then I am asked, "Why does there always seem to be a space that lacks equitable Black Fat Femme representation?" and my answer to that is always simple. That's because being Black, fat, and visibly queer isn't something that is profitable in most people's minds.

What's deeply concerning to me now more than ever is how so much of the Black Fat Femme representation is slowly going away because the powers that be don't find value in our stories. Moreover, the media has and continues to exploit our pain, and now that there are so many Black and queer folks openly writing about this (and their joy), the media has lost interest in our stories.

Media doesn't find capital in Black queer joy.

As I began outlining several of these chapters to highlight some of the folks who deeply impacted me, I began to realize that now there are so few Black Fat Femmes in media, leaving me baffled with how little progression we have made in the last few years when it comes to the inclusion of Black Fat Femme stories in media. If anything, a deeper part of me is concerned, considering how many people reach out to me telling me how alone they feel in their Black Fat Femme lived experience.

But, when I think about this and ponder why the media continues to omit our stories from the mainstream, I often think about Black Fat Femme joy, in all forms of representation, equated to resilience, agency, and freedom.

The heart of the matter is that we have – and continue – to live in a world where Black Fat Femme stories aren't uplifted because folk continue to fail to see the purpose our stories and our visibility serves. Even in telling my own story, I sometimes ask myself, "Why should anyone care about this?" knowing that even now – after years of being public about who I am and the person I am working to become – the industry is still telling me that my story doesn't matter.

But, I often remind people that it tells us that because of who I am.

I'm Black. I'm Fat. And I am Femme. These are three things that the world hates to see and wants to eradicate.

But what folks hate to see even more is Black Fat Femmes being represented in a way that depicts them as self-affirming victors in a world that is constantly reminding us to turn down our light.

I think about what being visibly queer means to me. Being openly me on the Internet and in the media is reminding someone they have the right to live. Being me openly in this world is in fact saving someone's life.

■ ■ ■

I'd be remiss if I didn't take this chance while talking about the importance of visibility to mention shows that have helped amplify Black Fat Femme stories. While I can stand on my soapbox for days talking about the ways the media needs to improve, I also want to recommend some of the shows and films that offered me purpose and helped me rediscover my power as a Black Fat Femme.

If we are going to talk about legends, there is no way I can't mention what I like to call my big three:

- Jennie Livingston's *Paris Is Burning*
- Elegance Bratton's docuseries *My House*
- Steven Canal's *Pose*

There have been several books by authors like my good friend Ricky Tucker, who wrote *And the Category Is: Inside New York's Vogue House and Ballroom Community*, which examines the importance of ball culture, and Tre'vell Anderson, who wrote *We See Each Other: A Black, Trans Journey Through TV and Film* that examines the implications of transgender representation in media and film.

For those who are not familiar, *Paris Is Burning* is a documentary that follows several folks who are active in the 1980s ball culture, an LGBTQ+ subculture that often centers around Black and Latinx people. Many of the words and language that I have to explain myself as a Black Fat Femme began with the exploration of this film and many of the people who are in it.

The film showed me the power of "owning my identity" in a way that didn't feel as performative as television, specifically noting that many Black television characters who are written or often coded as queer aren't queer in real life (yes, I am looking at you, *True Blood*).

In a world where I often felt so alone, *Paris Is Burning* told me that there were many people who looked and lived just like me, houseless, struggling to make ends meet, and trying to find joy in a space being celebrated for overcoming. That was beyond powerful for me.

This film helped me understand the importance of Black Fat Femmes having hopes and dreams, often in a world that doesn't give us space to do so. It also highlights how so many Black Fat Femmes live at the margins and why it is important for us to have community in moments where we are often (intentionally) left to our own demise.

The same can be said about both *Pose* and *My House*. Though I have written several articles on both of these shows and have interviewed the creators several times, there aren't enough words to explain how important these stories are to the lives of Black Fat Femmes.

For *Pose*, the show not only follows a Black trans woman taking in several Black and Latinx kids from the street, it helped me reframe what my definition of family was, especially after years of being so angry at my own family for the ways they treated me.

While many of the main characters of *Pose* weren't fat, they were in fact living at the margins of a late 1980s New York besieged with the AIDS epidemic, while also being underserved. Additionally, the show was able to paint an accurate depiction of the fight that Black Fat Femmes are up against when searching for justice, in addition to aiding themselves in searching for resources. The most important thing I always take away from this show is that my voice not only matters but I have to stay committed to speaking truth to power – even when my voice shakes a little.

Lastly, while *My House* never fully got the rightful praise it deserves as a beacon of positive Black Fat Femme representation, I still believe that this show illustrates how layered it is to be Black and queer.

In many of the participants of the docuseries, I found a lot of myself, because I, too, was going through so much change at that specific time of my life (while much of it was filmed in 2017, it premiered in 2018 on FUSE).

I saw myself in Precious Ebony who, like me, was searching for peace in their life. Moreover, they were searching to find a place to belong. While Precious found their community in the ball scene, it was affirming to see a Black Fat Femme actually be given space to not just exist but to thrive in the spaces that they do exist.

Knowing (and following) Precious now, it is affirming to know that even after years of struggling, they have garnered a following and the respect of those who see them as a legend in our world.

Each one of these stories gave a bit of life to me and my story and encouraged me to keep speaking truth to power.

Chapter 10

Yes, Black. Yes, Fat. Yes, Femme.

"There are fat Black (men) out here. They are in loving relationships. We are joyful. We are sexy. There is elegance and purity in our lives. I laugh my ass off every day."
—Jaquel Spivey

By now you've probably figured that much of this book is about giving the younger me a book that can be used as a roadmap to find self-love and validity. But it's also about those who are often left at the margins of the world, looking anywhere and everywhere to find some form of representation.

More than anything, this book is about giving folks the authority to use their words. To use words they may not have known or to use the words that they learned from reading this.

For many who either follow me on social media or know me beyond the para-social, this is something they often bring up. I have continued to give them language and an understanding of what it means to be marginalized, but more – how to own that experience and speak out about injustice.

As someone who often talks about what it was like for me to grow up in a world where I was not only silent but kept from knowing certain words, I write from that place of mind. I want you to know that it is okay for you to speak and say the thing. To name the thing. To own that feeling that comes with speaking your truth.

That is the through line of this book – how so many Black Fat Femmes in the media gave me the power to own my truth when I didn't know how. But now I do and I hope that you do too.

I want us to take pride in knowing that while the media often tries to paint a terrible portrait of Black Fat Femmes, there are so many who have rewritten that narrative for you. I want you to draw from your own inspirations and know that they, like you, had a story to tell – a story that might have helped you help someone else.

The key to all of our stories is that of survival. Yes, you – like me – might have felt alone and unmotivated to go on and then one day you saw someone who gave you a purpose to keep going.

Maybe this book is your purpose. I just hope you know that writing this book with you in mind is what gave me purpose.

I often think about the saying "They tried to bury us, but they didn't know that we were the seeds." I want folks to look at bits and pieces of my story as the nourishment you need to keep growing. Look out into your garden and see all the weeds, vines, and even the snakes in the grass and be happy that you still have something to work with. Like my mother would always tell me, "You might not have a lot, but at least you have something."

What would our lives be like if our ancestors never spoke up and taught others about systems of injustice? What if they never wrote about their experiences or even used their experiences to shape so many of the things I mention in this book such as the media I needed to stay alive?

Where would I be? Where would other Black Fat Femmes be?

What if I didn't have access to media that uplifted the voices of people like James Baldwin and Marsha P. Johnson. What if

I didn't have films like *Brother Outsider* that helped me shape my praxis for how I do social justice and talk about equity and advocacy in entertainment? Hearing Marsha P. Johnson say "Pay it no mind" really helped me understand that a lot of the contention people have around my Black Fat Femme identity really has nothing to do with me and everything to do with projection.

Writing this book in some way (and of course therapy) really helped me understand that much of the world's uncomfortability with my Black Fat Femmeness has to do with others and the way they learn about us – but more about what the world doesn't know about us.

Many of the images that the world gets of Black Fat Femmes are of folks who aren't as happy as I am to exist. They only see images of us living under the thumb of oppression and often vying for validation from people in this world who don't even see us as whole humans.

Moreover, I believe that my story and this book should encourage everyone to know that the only way to get free and from under the thumb of oppression is to be the person *you* want to be. You need to really accept the cards life has given you and remember that it's not about how many cards you do or don't have, it's that the ancestors have (and will continue) to teach us how to best play them.

■ ■ ■

Something that will forever be ingrained in my mind is the saying from Crissle West, "Words mean things." As much of this book is about representation, I do tend to stumble over my words when people ask me what this book is about and why it's needed.

Even though I spent so much of Chapter 9 talking about representation and the need for it in the media, I wanted to take the time to talk about why representation is needed in the world and why that word is so much more powerful than we give it credit for.

Merriam Webster defines representation as "a statement or account made to influence opinion or action." While there are multitudes of that definition, this is the one I like the most because that is truly what this book is about.

Action.

I want you to leave this book wanting to be a more true vision of yourself. To understand the risk that it takes to be your authentic self and to do it anyway. To recognize that people who tell you to shrink yourself are doing it only because they see your light and are intimidated by it. To recognize that the only way that systems of oppression can keep going is by someone bowing down and staying silent.

I wanted to write something that would inspire others to think about the people who have helped shape you or helped you stand taller, but more – to look to folks in the media who refused to not let their voices go unheard. To celebrate all that you are and all that you have to say.

To embrace the voices that speak loudly to your soul. The voices in the media that help you hold your head a little bit higher.

Growing up, people always said I talk too much – but now I think about everyone who has found their voices because of me using mine. That's the collective power we have as Black Fat Femmes.

This book also is about highlighting the issues that we have in the media around representation, especially when discussing Black Fat Femme representation. This book only scratches the surface when speaking about our representation, and if anything, it highlights the problems that live in media and how folks in power need to work to change it.

What's more important to name is how society often dismisses Black Fat Femme people from the center of their own stories and how often we are left out of important conversations. Even when trying to write this book, there were only a handful of Black Fat Femmes that I wanted to include who I truly felt are doing something right – living up to the definition of "representation."

As much as I needed that person (and this book) in this world to validate the younger me, writing and reflecting on many of my memories have solidified why I continue to write and talk openly about why other Black Fat Femmes are needed in the media.

It's about having access to a legacy that might provide you a roadmap to making hard decisions in your life. It's also about having a person or a character in your mind that you can have ancestral conversations with in order to keep existing in a world and system that was never built for you.

Being visibly you is tough, but there is someone out there who needs to see you. There is someone out there who needs to see *us*.

Now, before I dive deeper into the explanation of *why* being Black, fat, and visibly queer is more than necessary, now more than ever, I want to make sure I acknowledge that being visibly queer does come with some struggle and it's important to validate that. It would be silly of me to write a whole book talking about the importance of being visible without actually naming that standing in your truth is risky. It's also extremely taxing and might even cost you some opportunities and relationships.

Yes, Black. Yes, Fat. Yes, Femme.

Right before my grandfather passed away, he cut ties with me because he said that he could not be associated with someone "like me." I have also had friends tell me that the way I present makes them uncomfortable and have had them retract our friendship when I came out as nonbinary trans.

I have even been fired from a job because me being visibly queer "didn't align with [my employer's] mission."

What has been most hurtful is the ways media has treated me for being vocal about lived experience and the lack of representation I continue to see. I have lost opportunities for calling out transphobia. I have had folks take me off of projects because they said I kept pushing "an LGBTQ+ agenda."

But they were right. Me being authentically myself, authentically Black Fat and Femme, is about a bigger mission. It's a mission to keep other Black Fat Femmes alive long enough to know that their lives are worth living.

Yes, being visible, in any regard, as a marginalized person is a risk – but it is a risk that many of us need to take because our ancestors remind us of what's at stake if we don't. Some of the folks I mentioned earlier in this book might have had to shrink themselves to survive. But that's the thing, they wanted *US to not just survive, but live in abundance.*

I want to acknowledge that being proud of who you are takes a lot of gumption. But it also takes reflection and knowing that you have legions of people behind you, lifting you up as you stand tall.

I know it can feel like you are bringing unwanted attention to yourself, and you might even ask yourself why anyone might want to put themselves through all that. It's knowing that in being authentically you, you are affirming that your existence is in fact resistance, and that in itself is mighty.

Sure, there are days I have had to push through being *visibly me* in moments that I didn't have the energy. Much of how I feel is in fact battle fatigue. There are days I swap my heels for sandals because I don't want people staring at me trying to figure out my gender. There are days that I have gone out of my way to find a gender-neutral bathroom in an airport because I didn't want to have to scream, "Mind your business!" to the man policing what bathroom I use.

And there are days I tuck my hands into my pocket to hide my nails so I don't have to worry about being misgendered.

These are all valid reasons to not be visible. However, regardless of how you show up, white supremacy and patriarchy are silently laughing in the background watching you fade away. When you recognize that these systems are working to make *you* tired of *you*, it changes the ways you think about being visible.

Understand that these systems are working to silence you in order to oppress you.

Being visible in any regard means recognizing the battle and still showing up anyway. It's recognizing that even in the days you do tuck yourself away, said systems of oppression are dancing around you hoping that others will take notice and do the same. But it's the moments that you are visibly you – no matter in what context – that tells others that they have a right to exist.

I often think about a moment years back when my partner and I went to Disneyland (a place we often frequent) and had a moment that told me that being visible is in fact changing people's lives. When we were walking toward the entrance, we saw a Black family take their child out of the car. As we walked by holding hands, the mother and the child stopped what they

Yes, Black. Yes, Fat. Yes, Femme.

were doing, smiled at us, waved, and continued about their business.

There was another moment where I was at the Grove in Los Angeles, California, with my partner, and a Black family ran up to me and shared that they listen weekly to my show. The mother went on to say that they love everything I am doing and appreciated how much I have put myself – and my life – out in public for other Black queer people to see.

For some, these moments are just moments for me to wax my car and talk about how "amazing" my work is. But the truth of the matter is that it's never been about me. It's knowing that by being Black, fat, and visibly queer, I am doing the same thing that so many other Black Fat Femmes have done for me.

It's affirming that while there might be people in this world who may not want to see you, there are folks like me working to offer you the biggest mirror so you not only can see your reflection but fully like and love the reflection that you see.

There is so much power in being visible, not just because others are able to see you, but it allows you to see the work you've done to love you fully formed.

So now you're probably wondering, "Well how does one get to a place where they are comfortable with being visibly queer?" That, my friend, isn't something I can truly explain to you in a chapter.

Much of my "visibility" came from recognizing that there was never going to be anyone who would represent me the way I wanted to represent me. I knew the world would be okay with me and my stories being swallowed up if I didn't share them.

I even think about the years (yes, years) that it took to get this book published. There were numerous people who told me – both in writing and to my face – that there isn't a market for a book about the experiences of Black Fat Femme people. There were also people who told me that my podcast with the same theme wouldn't sell either.

I am forever thankful to IHeartMedia for picking it up.

But I want to acknowledge the power that is being visible. You have power in existing when you are being authentically you.

This idea of "power" isn't something that I just happened to stumble upon. It's a callback to many of the wonderful meetings I had with my therapist who helped me reframe the thought of visibility and representation.

I can recall sitting with her and talking to her about a time I was at a bag carousel at LAX and a group of young people were staring at me and laughing. I went on to explain to her that in that moment, I was taken back to my younger years where I was teased for showing up "like a girl" and how tired I was of people who didn't even know me – or my journey – making fun of me.

She then looked up from her notepad and asked, "Was there ever a time in your life where you thought of that as your superpower?"

I was befuddled because I didn't know how to respond. I sat there for a minute processing what she had just said to me because it didn't make sense. After almost 15 minutes of me talking about this moment and all the terrible memories it brought up, how in the hell did we get to talking about *superpowers*?

I processed it. "No. . .," I responded.

My therapist then went on to explain the importance of reframing – and how so much of who I am as a Black Fat Femme is in fact a superpower, because I have the ability to show people what freedom looks like. Moreover, I also have

205

the ability to make people stop in their tracks and question their own existence – something that I had never thought about.

I was blown away by this idea because up to this moment I had never thought of myself as powerful. After further reflecting on this conversation, it helped me to understand the power of visibility and helped me get to this place where I was able to actively see my Black Fat Femme identity as not just something I loved but as a God-given superpower.

So, here we are. Keep embracing the power of your story, and remember that there are so many people in this world who don't just need to see you but need to *hear* you. You simply speaking up for yourself and owning who you are is in fact the catalyst for change and is what makes both you and our world a better place.

This is my gift to you: a reminder that your voice, your existence, and your lived experience are, in fact, your greatest strengths. In a world that often tries to silence or overlook Black Fat Femmes, never forget the profound impact of you being visibly you.

Acknowledgments

To my lord and savior Beyoncé Giselle Knowles Carter: I know you may never read this, but thank you for reminding me how much "Bigger" I am and how good it feels to "Be Alive." Your music, your creativity, and your existence has inspired me more than you will ever know, and I pray for the day I get to tell you this in person. You are the reason why I truly keep going.

To my *Black therapist*: You truly have helped me make so much of this life and have really helped me find the beauty in being a Black Fat Femme. Thank you for always helping understand that I am the gift and that I am so much more than the world gives me credit for. I couldn't forget to thank you because this book wouldn't be a thing without your push.

To Mayhem Miller and Latrice Royale: Thank you for being a beautiful example of what perseverance looks like. Thank you for existing, and thank you for never letting the world stop you from being the most amazing representation of drag and Black queer people. You two will *always* and *forever* be my favorite drag queens, and I am so glad that I get to tell you that both of your legacies are what inspired me to write this book.

To my family, specifically my momma (aka my favorite lady): Thank you for always seeing me and trying to understand me even when you didn't know how. You have always been the wind beneath my wings, and even though it was a hell of a ride to get here, I am thankful that I had such a beautiful, strong, and loving mother. I will say this until the end of time: you are the best mother anyone could ask for, and I am so thankful I got you in this lifetime.

Justin (aka Bubba), Valerie, and Grayson: Y'all will always be the people I do this for. You continue to remind me why I do what I do and why I will never stop doing it. I love you for always being there for me.

To my partner, Jonathan Ray: You are the reason this book exists. You reminded me, often, that I had a story to tell, and I am so thankful for you in both my life and in my creative processes and for being part of my story. Thank you for always giving me space to be big, small, and everything in between. You continue to add so much joy to my life, and I am so glad that I get to spend this timeline with you. Mucho baby kisses.

Dorothy: I remember when I told you I sold the book and you damn near cried. Thank you for always being so proud of me, for showing up for me, and for being my designated godmother. I love you more than you could ever know.

Giselle Phelps: Whew. What a moment. Thank you for always being the first person to tell me that it's possible. Thank you for reminding me what I am worth, and thank you for always reminding me that I deserve more. You truly were the best agent anyone could ask for, and I am so thankful for all that you continue to do – not just for me – but for the world.

To my manager, Stephanie: Your baby is a published author. Thank you for always reminding me that my words are my superpower. We got next, and I am so blessed to have you on this journey with me. Love you forever and ever.

To my team over at iHeartMedia, specifically Will Pearson: From the day we met, you told me I was gonna be a star. I still don't believe you, but I am so thankful you saw my shine and continue to see it. Thank you for being the best chosen uncle I could ever ask for.

To Anna Hosnieh and Joelle Smith, who made my show a reality and encouraged me to get this proposal and book done: Thank you. I wouldn't have listened to you otherwise until you told me that day at Pod Movement that I had something special – both with this show and with the book. You two have truly been my North Star, and I thank you for hearing me *and* seeing me.

To my cohost and sister, Jordan Daniels: B*tch. We are finally here. Ever since 2016 we have been riding for each other, and I will always thank you for being the one person to tell me to get my big ass up and keep going on the days that it feels impossible. Also thank you for being the bestest friend and cohost I could ever ask for.

To those who support the *Black, Fat, Femme* podcast: Just. Thank. You. Thank you for tuning in, writing in, and constantly pushing us to create a show that celebrates the intersections of identity. We love you and thank you for always giving us a platform to be ourselves on the show.

To Dr. James Simmons, my ace boon coon: I will forever hold our friendship close to my heart because in the moments I feel alone and lost in this world/industry, you always pull me back. I am so grateful our stars crossed, and I can't wait until the day that we are toasting on the red carpet together. Know that I see you and thank you for blessing my world with your friendship.

Jessica Marie Garcia: Girl. How many times have I called you crying about this industry and you told me to Echa Pa'lante? Thank you for teaching me what real friends in this industry are, and thank you for allowing me to be part of your family. I love you to the moon.

Jimanieka: Let me tell you something – God knew to connect us back at CSUSB, and I am so glad he/she/they did. Thank you for always being the family I have always wanted. Knowing that I can count on you means more to me than you will ever know.

Raaya and Scentoria: Thank you for 20+ years of laughs, friendship, and love. God honestly directed me to y'all, and I am so glad we get to walk this earth on the same timeline. Now stop sending me pictures of *food*! (I love you!)

Joy, Piya, Dr. James, DJ Kelly, Sam and Matt: You've been with me from the beginning. Thank you for never leaving me behind after the field of Student Affairs did. Now who's calling WHO?

Big Reesha Howard: You have always seen it for me, encouraged me, and lifted me up. Thank you for always having my back and reminding me that I am so much more than what the world gives me credit for. So much of this book is because of you and our long talks. I love you more than words can detail.

My boo Darell Hunt.: God really was looking out for me the day I came across your video on Facebook. I am so glad that I have a friend, a sister, and a true ride-or-die in you. Thank you for always being there for me in my time of need. This is for us!

Heather and Qasim: Thank you for showing me the true meaning of friendship. This is also for you.

Angela, Ericka (and Dasa!), Ingrid, and Yuli: Thank you for always believing in me and encouraging me. I wouldn't have ever thought I had a story to tell without all of you encouraging me. Thank you for always reminding me that I am so much bigger than the world gives me credit for.

My chosen family members: Simen, Diana, Leta, Louie and Gia, Walter, Matt, Angie, Heather, Gary, Daniel, Amy and Isaac, Lisa and Charlie, Bernadette, Kyle, Jared, Jarrett (with two t's),

Tre'vell, Shar, Tennessee, Gabe, Toi, Benita Gus, Jacob, Parker, Micah, Dr. Torie, Gayle, Omar and Brianna, Phelan, Avery, Loren, Penelope and Elias, Saff and Addy, Chris Bauman, the entire Fowler family, and Tariq and my entire Camp Pride Family (delfin, Katie and Lisa, Jae, Eddie, Don . . . that-Don-da-Don-Don-Don!): Thank you. I look to each of you as inspirations in so many different ways, and I can't thank you enough for always reminding me how talented, smart, and inspirational I am – even when I don't believe it.

My team at APB: Thank you for supporting me and keeping the lights on. I wouldn't have a fraction of my success without your support.

Everyone at Wiley Global: Thank you for believing in me and my voice. After years of being told that my story didn't matter, thank you for proving it did.

To the Black Fat Femmes who have always felt overlooked, unworthy, and unloved: This book is for you. Know I see us and love us always.

To everyone else who I love that I forgot to mention: Blame it on my head and not my heart. Know I love and appreciate you too and won't forget to thank you in the second book!

I love us for real.

About the Author

Dr. Jonathan P. Higgins (DoctorJonPaul) is an award-winning educator, professor, national speaker, freelance journalist, thought leader, and media critic who examines the intersections of identity, gender, and race in entertainment. Named National Black Justice Coalition's Inaugural Emerging Leaders to Watch and *Business Equality Magazine*'s "Top 40 LGBTQ People Under 40," their work has been featured on sites like Essence, Ebony, Complex, MTV NEWS, Out Magazine, BET, and Entertainment Weekly. A Culture Strike 2021 Disruptor, Black Boy/Girl Writes Fellow, and Twitter Spaces Spark Creator, Dr. Higgins is a trailblazer who is creating, sharing, and crafting the stories their ancestors didn't get to tell.

Dr. Higgins is currently the inaugural Director of Strategic Media & Advocacy for Rainbow Pride Youth Alliance and has held positions at both Chernin Entertainment & Edith Productions. They have consulted with multiple brands on inclusion projects including United Artists, Amazon Prime, Fox, the NFL, Apple, Disney, Instagram, Buzzfeed, Gay and Lesbian Alliance Against Defamation (G.L.A.A.D.), and Ulta Beauty.

They have also been a featured speaker for South by Southwest (SXSW) and TEDx and most recently was the first Black queer person to be a featured speaker at ForbesBLK. You can also see them on hit shows like Netflix's *Nailed It* and Fuse's *Like a Girl*.

They are the creator, executive producer, and host of the *Black, Fat, Femme* podcast, which was developed via iHeartMedia's Next Up Initiative in 2021. The podcast has gone on to be named one of the "top Black podcasts to listen to" by both *Ebony* and *Pride Magazine*, was a Webby Award honoree, and won a Shorty Award for best Lifestyle & Entertainment podcast.

Dr. Higgins holds a doctorate of Educational Leadership in Social Justice from the University of Redlands, being named as a distinguished recipient of the School of Education's Centennial Excellence Award in 2024.

They continue to write and lecture regularly on what liberation means for Black, fat, queer, and nonbinary individuals and what folks can do to better show up for those who are often left at the margins in media and education.

Index

A

Abercrombie era, 112

Acceptance, journey/search, 99, 112, 177–178

"Act like a man," need, 3

Adam4Adam.com (app), 78, 79

Addiction, conversation, 109

Agency
    receiving, 146
    reclamation, 169

Aggression, promotion, 30

America's Next Top Model (ANTM) (show), 51–53, 64, 145, 147, 151
    journey, 152

AMPM food, obsession, 46–47

Anderson, Tre'vell, 193

And the Category Is: Inside New York's Vogue House and Ballroom Community (Tucker), 193

Anger
    impact, 39–40
    suppression, 83

Anti-Blackness, 113–114, 139–140, 161, 184

Anxiety, cycle, 161

Arsenio Hall Show, 26

Attractiveness, benchmark, 131

Audacity, 11, 169
    authenticity, relationship, 168

Authenticity, 170–177
    commitment, 150
    definition, understanding, 163
    fear, relationship, 164–165
    idea, redefining, 162
    legacy, 149–150
    redefining, 159
    term, feeling, 163–164
    worthiness, recognition, 177–178

Authentic self
    becoming, 67
    being, 161
    embracing, 168–171, 173
    encouragement, 68
    risk, 200

Authority figures, opinion, 21

B

"Baby One More Time..."
(Spears), 37
Backhanded compliments, 77
Bad bitch(ery), 141, 156, 158
Baldwin, James, 7, 144, 198
Banks, Tyra, 51, 65
Baptism, coercion, 43–44
Beauty/desirability, media
definitions, 129–130
Beauty standards, conforming,
132
Belonging, sense, 98
Bigotry, 169, 176
Bitch, becoming, 139, 142, 148
Black children, adultification, 3
Black Fat Femme
access, absence, 189
advocacy, 184–185
affirmation, 54
Black boy identification, 33
celebration, 12–13
confidence, 148
craft, seriousness, 118
existence, validation, 191
experience, discussion, 18
feeling, 8, 68–69, 143
flowers, taking, 147
identity
ownership, 142
perception, 206
interaction, 10, 62
issues, examination
(reasons), 57

journey, 27, 55, 152
media perception, 56
media portrait, 198
mental/physical pain, 28
misconception, 162–163
pain, experiencing, 23
performance, 32, 69
positive representation,
absence, 129
power, 142, 154
problem, coded messages
(impact), 75
receiving/respecting,
demands, 95–96
representation,
disappearance, 191
silencing/overlooking, 206
societal dismissal, 201
stereotypes, 74
stories, inclusion/
amplification, 191–193
struggles, 187–188
survival, 160
treatment, 117
uncomfortability, 199
visibility, frustration, 77
Blackness
control, absence, 113
gender, performance, 41
societal attitudes, 171–172
Black queer stories,
importance, 183
Black representation,
existence, 188

Black Student Alliance, 182

Blanks, Billy, 107

Bob the Drag Queen, blogger
post reactions, 165

Body
hatred, growth, 124–125
hiding, difficulty, 123–124
resentment, 153
shaming, pervasiveness, 167

Bratton, Elegance, 193

Brother Outsider (movie), 199

Bullying, target, 2–3

"Butching" up, 91

C

Campbell, Naomi, 54

Canal, Steven, 193

Character
loving, 134
strength, 166

Chester, Rodney, 137

Chiffon, chronicles, 35

Christian character, performance,
37

Cisgender men
hatred, 82
hostility, 91–92
opportunities, 88
prettiness, appearance, 98

Classes, skipping, 72

Coaching, 148–149

Collective resilience, fostering, 169

Color Purple, The (movie), 181

Comic View (BET), 26

Coming-out moment, 66

Coming-out revolution, 63

Coming-out season, 59–60

Community
observation, ability, 157
search, 112

Compton Cafeteria Riots, 165

Conforming, societal
pressures, 149

Contact lenses, usage, 85–86

"Cool" aesthetic, retail store
usage, 131

COVID-19 pandemic, impact, 107

Craig, Jenny, 26

Creativity (spark), representation
(impact), 186

Crenshaw, Kimberlé, 13, 62

Cult upbringing, 159

D

Dance, representation
(dialogues), 167–168

Death threats, 49

Deen, Paula, 106

Defiance, 176

Depression, 26–27, 49, 161

Desserts, eating, 111

Destiny's Child, 139

Dickenson, Janice, 65

Diggs, Taye, 132

Discrimination, 13, 176

Disdain, experience, 31

Disneyland, visit, 203–204

Documentation, creation, 8

Dominance, promotion, 30
DragCon, announcement, 119
Drag Race. See RuPaul's
   Drag Race

E
Effeminacy, teasing, 124
Ellen (show), 63
Embarrassment, origin, 122
Emotional detachment,
   promotion, 30
Emotional unavailability,
   struggle, 88
Emotions
   protection, 144
   validity, acknowledgement, 177
Empowerment, commitment, 150
Environmental safety, feeling
   (luxury), 2
Eurocentric beauty standards,
   conforming (societal
   expectation), 172
Existence, fear (emotion), 145
Eye, story initiation, 3

F
Facebook, 94, 179
Fag, naming, 39–40
Family
   escape, 66
   memories, food (relationship),
      105–106
   treatment, 18

Fashion bullies, impact, 54
Fashion Queens (show), 95
Fat
   avoidance, 104
   calling, 3
   shaming, 104
Fat person (people)
   emotions, protection, 144
   villianization, 184
Fatphobia, 48, 141
   experiencing, 78
   issues, 5, 9, 157
   pervasiveness, 167
   presence, 114
   understanding, 76
   undoing, 12
Fear, 64
   authenticity, relationship,
      164–165
   impact, 147–148, 164
Feelings
   ownership, 197
   sharing, 79
Femininity
   perception, 89
   societal attitudes, 171–172
Femmephobia, 56, 141
   experiencing, 78
   issues, 5, 9
   presence, 60
   understanding, 76
   undoing, 12
Fifth-grade bathroom, fight, 4

Food
    addiction, 109–110, 125
    impacts, 105–107
    obsession, 103–105
    processing levels, impact, 109
    relationship, problem, 102
Franklin, Aretha, 118
Frustration, sharing, 189

G
Ganache, Silky Nutmeg, 166–167
Gay.com (social media), 68,
    78, 129
Gay porn, sneak-watching, 47
Gay Straight Alliance, 128, 182
Gender
    binaries, conforming (societal
        expectation), 172
    concept, 84–85
    construction, 81
    constructs, presence, 89
    identity, 24, 52, 91, 148
    mask, wearing, 90–91
    performance, 87
        religious teachings, 41
    politics, 86
Gibson, Lauireann, 72
Girl songs, singing, 1
Gone with the Wind (movie), 162
Good Hair (movie), 94, 95
Gospel According to André, The
    (documentary), 57
Grindr (app), 78, 113

H
Happiness
    difficulty, 8–9
    worthiness, recognition,
        177–178
Harm, origin, 157
Hatred
    experience, 78
    knowledge, 45
Hegemonic masculinity, idea
    (exaggeration), 82
Heteronormative ideals,
        conforming (societal
        expectation), 172
Heteronormativity, 84
Heterosexual archetype, media
    perpetuation, 56
Higgins/Derek J (conference
    attendance photo), 99
Higgins/Ms. Lawrence
    (ForbesBLK attendance
    photo), 100
Higgins/Royale (DragCon
    attendance photo),
    120
Homophobia, problem, 125,
    157, 185
Honesty, demand, 174
Houston, Whitney, 36
Human experience,
    richness/diversity
    (recognition), 169
Hurt, feeling, 31

Hypermasculinity, 82,
    125, 161
Hypermasculinized men, need
    (misunderstanding), 83

I

Identity
    complexities, 172
    embracing, 151
    engagement, inability, 65
    politics, performance, 41
    problem, 123
    societal fixation, 23
IHeartMedia, 205
"I'm Every Women"
    (Houston), 36
Inadequacy, feelings,
    131–132
Inclusivity, dialogues,
    167–168
Individuality, strength, 166
Inside Edition (show), 114
Internal bias, 74–75
Internal dialogue, fueling, 76
Internalized racism,
    113–114, 151
Intersectional experience,
    loneliness, 185
Intersectional identities, 6, 157
Intersectionality, 13, 62, 76,
    122–123
Intersectional politics,
    awakening, 116
Isolation, moments, 42

J

Jackson, Michael R., 190
Jehovah Witnesses, 19, 21, 42–45
    escape, 66
    organization, return, 50
Jenny Jones (show), 35–36, 63,
    180
Jerry Springer (show), 36, 180
Johnson, Marsha P., 6, 165, 198
Jokes, harm (uncomprehension),
    96
Judgement, facing, 168
Junk food, consumption, 125

K

Kenti episode, 52
Kieth, Gregory, 134
King, Jr., Martin Luther, 165
Kings of Comedy, The, 25

L

LaLa Ri, blogger post reactions,
    165
Latch-key kids, 20
Laughter, 87
Leno, Jay, 26
Lesbian, Gay, Bisexual, or
    Transgender (LGBTQ+)
    people, discussion,
    19–20
Letting go, learning, 153
LGBTQ+
    agenda, pushing, 202
    characters, immersion, 51

people, meeting, 133
subculture, focus, 193
LGBTQ+ community, 124
navigation, 62
queen, naming, 59
treatment, 69
Life
acceptance, 199
building, 151
change, 139
lesson, 146
wanting/needing, demand, 155
Lifestyle, choice, 42
Livingston, Jennie, 193
Loneliness, feelings, 42, 94, 128
Looks/appearance, hatred, 126
Lorde, Audre, 6, 144
Love, 121
absence, 132–133
discovery/search, 12, 78, 112,
128, 135–136
display, 151
need, 46
themes, exploration, 30
ubiquity, 64
LoveBScott.com, 97
Luther: Never Too Much
(documentary), 23

M

Macroaggressiveness, 95
Mad TV (show), 75
Making the Band (show),
71–76, 79

Manhood, 25, 88–89
Manly actions, 86–87
Marginalization, societal
prejudice/personal
experiences, 171
Marginalized communities,
solidarity/empowerment
(encouragement), 169
Marginalized person, visibility
(risk), 202
Masculine appearance,
desperation, 84
Masculinity
display, refusal, 79
emulation, 16–17
expectations, problem, 2
performance, importance,
36–37
safety, feeling (absence), 90
stereotypes, beating, 32
Masks, wearing, 90
Matthews, Stacy Layne, 116
Maury Povich (show), 63, 180
Mayfield, Dexter, 7, 167–168
Media
Black Fat Femme stories,
inclusion, 191
influence, pervasiveness, 132
junkie, behavior, 91
messages, impact, 48
power, 180–181
problems, 189
representation, 179
issues, 200–201

Memories, 28–29
Mental health, checking,
        122–123
Microaggression, 163
Microaggressiveness, 95
Miller, Mayhem, 7, 166
Misgendering, 203
Misogynoir (hatred of Black
        women), 126, 161
Mitchum, Preston, 191
Mother, comparison (pain),
        61–62
My House (Bratton), 193–194
My So Called Life (show), 47
Myspace.com (social media), 68,
        94, 129, 179
Mystique (drag queen),
        115–116

N
Nails, intentionality, 87
Narrative, rewriting, 198
Nigger, calling, 1–3
Noah's Arc (show), 133–136, 187
Nonbinary, meaning, 92
Nunn, Laurie, 186

O
Openness, themes
        (exploration), 30
Oppression, 161
    backlash, 11
    impact, 54, 122–123

magnitude, 6
objection, 157
Overeating, 46–47
Ozempic, craze, 114

P
Pain, undoing, 39
Paris Is Burning? (Livingston),
        183, 193
People
    judgement, 5
    pleaser role, emptiness,
        160
Performance
    importance, 32
    questions, 20
    watching, 33
Personal power, 173
Physical appearance,
        popularity/self-worth
        (connection), 131
Polk, Patrik-Ian, 134
Pop culture, immersion, 63
Porter, Dawn, 23, 27
Pose (Canal), 193, 194
Power
    idea, 205
    reclamation, 169
    relinquishment, 168
Precious Ebony, 195
Prejudice/bigotry,
        collective resilience
        (fostering), 169

Privilege, result, 13
Projection, problems, 154
Project, term (usage), 14

Q
Queen
    being, 61–62, 70
    creation, 59
    internal bias, 74–75
    labeling, 60
"Queen Kong," 57
Queer as Folk (show), 48,
        51, 63, 132
Queer cisgender Black man,
        discussion, 84
Queer English lesson, 60
Queerness, 162
    conditioning, 18
    control, absence, 113
    fear, 30–31
    freezing, 90–91
    hiding, 44–45
    remarks, 95
    societal attitudes,
        171–172
    visibility, 201
        comfort, 204–205
Queerphobia, media
        (impact), 57
Queer powerhouses,
        impact, 148
Queer representation,
        existence, 188

Queer spaces, experience,
        112, 116
Queer television, sneaking/
        watching, 63

R
Race, negotiation, 52
Racism, 185
    experiencing, 78
    impact, 112, 157
    issues, 5, 9
    media, impact, 57
    undoing, 12
Radical self-love, concept,
        143–144
Rage, struggle, 88
"Ready to fight," 4
Real Housewives of Atlanta
        (show), 93, 95
Reality, perception, 64
Relationship, tumult, 27–28
Religion
    escape, 66
    impact, 161
Religious ideals, problems, 41
Representation
    absence, 202
    accuracy, ensuring,
        182–183
    definition, 200
    impact, 186
    media issues, 200–201
    need, 200

Representation/exposure, importance, 10
Residual self-hatred, 6
Resilience, 163
  cultivation, authenticity (usage), 177
  legacy, 149–150
Ricki Lake (show), 35–36, 63
Rivera, Sylva, 6
Royale, J. Latrice, 7, 10, 114, 117–118
  performance, 118–119
  validation, 119–120
RuPaul, media representation, 189–190
RuPaul's Drag Race (RPDR) (show), 114–117, 165–166, 190
  Snatch Game episode, 117–118
Rustin, Bayard, 7, 165

S
Sadness
  cessation, desire, 45
  moments, 142
Saint Laurent, Yves, 57
Savage, Dan, 65
Scruff (app), 78, 113
Self-acceptance, 149
  audacity, 169
Self-blame, avoidance, 169
Self-compassion, vulnerability/ resilience, 172

Self-consciousness, 15, 121–122
Self-discovery, journey, 9, 99, 154, 171, 177–178
Self-doubt, 142
Self-empowerment, journey, 177
Self-hatred, 65, 76, 126
  understanding, 129
  unlearning, 6–7, 19
Self-love, 170
  discovery, 197
  journey, 9, 154
  meaning, 137
  trail, 8
  transformative power, 150
Self-reflection, themes (exploration), 30
Sex Education (Nunn), 186
Sex in the City (show), 70
Sexism, 84
  presence, 60
Sexuality
  insinuation, 17
  interrogation, 21
  questions, 20
  speculations, 19
  struggles, 25–26
Sexual object, queer men treatment, 136–137
Sexual racism, 56
Shade, throwing, 77
Shame, 64–65
Shepard, Matthew, 48–49

Sizeism, media (impact), 57, 148
Size, thought/obsession, 111
Smith, Anna Nicole, 130
Social justice, 199
Social media
  following, 197
    absence, 117
    influencers, rise, 131
Social validation, popularity/
    self-worth (connection), 131
Societal norms
  challenge, 98, 150
  impact, 149
Softness
  concept, 29
  perception, 38
  struggle, 30
Space, reclamation, 149
Spears, Britney, 37
Sports, participation (forcing), 101–102
Stephens, Darryl, 134
Stereotypes
  destruction, 148
  media, impact, 68–69
  playing out, 74
Stonewall Riots, 165
Superpowers, discussion, 205–206
"Superwomen" (White), 1
Systemic oppression, struggle, 175

T
Tae Bo (Blanks), 107
Talley, André Leon, 7, 10, 51–55, 143
  awe, 145
  observation, 70
  shame, 56–57
  world response, 64
Television, impact, 36
Testosterone, usage, 127
Therapy, usage, 108, 139–140, 143–144, 187
This Boy's Life (movie), 183–184
Thriving, 187
  concept/alienness, 98
TMZ (show), 114
Torment, worsening, 40
Toxic masculinity, 38
Transphobia, 184, 185
Trauma, 160
  bonding/reliving, issues, 4
True Blood, 193
True self, being (idea), 164
Truth
  conveyance, 152
  speaking, 197
Tucker, Ricky, 193

U
Ugliness, 121–122
Undressed (show), 47, 64
Uniqueness, embracing, 152
Uno (game), 142–143

V

Validation, 119–120

Vandross, Jr., Luther Ronzoni, 16

Vandross, Luther, 15–17, 20–22, 24–26

jokes, 27

joy, 30

life, examination, 32–33, 70

performance, watching, 33–34

softness, 29–30

Visceral hatred, impact, 40–41

Visibility

battle, recognition, 203

importance, 149–150, 176, 191–193, 201

power, 204

acknowledgement, 205

pushing, 203

risk, 202

Voice(s)

amplification, 184

inclusivity, 189

validation, 180

Vulnerability, 30

demand, 174

W

Weight

fluctuation, 26

obsession, 129–131

teasing, 108

Weight-loss products, celebrity endorsement, 130

Well-being, interest (absence), 24

We See Each Other: A Black, Trans Journey Through TV and Film (Anderson), 193

West, Crissle, 199

White, Karyn, 1

Whiteness, emphasis (attractiveness benchmark), 131

White queerness, 56

White supremacy, appearance/manifestation, 140

Will and Grace (show), 48, 51, 70, 132, 185

Williams, Jason, 72–78

life, fixation, 79

Williams, Wendy, 17

Winfrey, Oprah, 20, 119

Women

societal hatred, 89

violence, stigma, 30

Words

meaning, 199

usage, authority, 197

X

Xanga (social media), 68, 73

XY.com, 129

Y

Young social media, 68